D0917632

BEING OUR
HIGHER SELVES

— Guide to a Fulfilling Life —

BEING OUR HIGHER SELVES

— Guide to a Fulfilling Life —

Selected from the Writings of
SRI CHINMOY

BEING OUR HIGHER SELVES

— Guide to a Fulfilling Life —

Selected from the Writings of
Sri Chinmoy

Sri Chinmoy's first book, *Meditations: Food for the Soul,* was published in 1970.

Copyright © August 27, 2021 Sri Chinmoy Centre

ISBN 978-1-945758-07-2

Compiled by Bhadra P. Kleinman, Ph.D.

Cover photograph shows Sri Chinmoy in 1985, and was taken by Bhashwar Hart.

All rights reserved. No portion of this book may be reproduced without express written permission from the Publisher. Printed in the U.S.A.

Manifestation-Glow Press
84-71 Parsons Boulevard
Jamaica, New York 11432

Table of Contents

Editor's Preface

Introduction: The Heart

Chapter 1: Humility

Chapter 2: Positivity

Chapter 3: Kindness, Concern, Sympathy, Compassion

Chapter 4: Love/Oneness

Love

Oneness

Chapter 5: Self-Giving

Chapter 6: Forgiveness

Chapter 7: Gratitude

About the Author

Endnotes

Editor's Preface

Wherever you go, go with inspiration and aspiration.
Whatever you do, do with love and concern.
Whomever you see, see with purity's beauty
and responsibility's glory.[1]

We all wish to have relationships that are satisfying, supportive, and filled with delight. But, hard as we try, at times we seem to be unable to make that happen. We simply do not know what to do. The teachings of Sri Chinmoy offer us considerable guidance in getting ourselves on the path to our best selves. For a future of hope, fulfilment and universal oneness, we must learn to look deep within and discover and cultivate our aspiration and our highest inner capacities. As Sri Chinmoy says:

"This world of ours has two choices: one is to establish friendship, brotherhood and oneness. Another is to try to conquer or destroy others. When we adopt the second approach, ultimately, we destroy ourselves. What we, as human beings, actually want is joy, happiness and satisfaction. These qualities we can only get by uniting ourselves with other human beings. These human beings are nothing but an extension of our own reality. When we establish our oneness with the rest of the world-family, we get joy and this joy lasts forever. But when we conquer someone by using superior strength and power, by hook or by crook, we cannot get permanent joy. Only through union do we get joy, not by division. When we extend ourselves, when we spread our wings and claim the whole world as our own, very own, when we love Mother Nature, then the joy that we get will be everlasting. And this joy has in it sweetness, tremendous sweetness. We are longing for this joy, the joy of the creation."[2]

The following selections, drawn from a wide variety of Sri Chinmoy's over 1600 books, provide the inspiration, instruction and practical advice that will lead us towards better human relationships. Here we focus on some of the most helpful of all qualities – humility, positivity, kindness, love, forgiveness, self-giving and gratitude. As we learn to bring these supremely good ways of being to the fore, we will find our lives, and the lives of those we care about, becoming increasingly satisfying and fulfilling.

On a personal note: In choosing selections, I was thinking about students of Sri Chinmoy's; and about readers who are unfamiliar with his writings, but wish to learn from them. For the first group, I chose selections that seemed designed to help us in our efforts to bring our daily behaviors up to a higher standard. For the second, when possible I chose writings that are easy to understand, and tried to organize them in a clear and easy to follow format. Except for the chapter- and sub-headings, every word in this book was written by Sri Chinmoy, and published in the sources listed. However, in the attempt to make the selected passages concise and understandable, I shortened some selections. Readers who wish to know the entire context of each passage are strongly encouraged to consult the primary sources, which can be accessed on www.srichinmoylibrary.com and in the original print books.

Joy, as well as needed illumination, came to me while I was working on this book. I wish to thank Nilima Silver, who critiqued the first version; to thank Pratibha Agdern, Nayana Hein, Sutushti Lang, and Hladini Wilson who unstintingly offered important ideas for the improvement of earlier versions; and to thank Ranjana K. Ghose who has provided inspired leadership to the Sri Chinmoy Centre in the years since Sri Chinmoy's passing. With all my heart I am grateful to Sri Chinmoy for his decades of service to the cause of world peace and for his transformational contributions to my little life.

Bhadra P. Kleinman, Ph. D.

Introduction

THE HEART

The Heart and Love

When I am
Inside my heart,
It is all compassion,
Concern and love.[1]

The heart is like a fountain of peace, joy and love. You can sit at the base of the fountain and just enjoy.[2]

The world exists just because love still exists on earth. If this one divine quality left the world, then there could be no existence on earth. No other divine quality can create, sustain and fulfil God here on earth like the quality of love. Divine love does not mean an emotional exchange of human thoughts or ideas, but it means the fulfilment of oneness.[3]

The heart knows how to identify itself with others' hearts. The mother does not have to show her love for her child by saying, "I love you, I love you," because the mother's identification with the child makes the child feel that he is loved. The real heart does not need to convince; it has the power of oneness.[4]

If you concentrate on your heart and soulfully repeat a few times, "Love, love, love," then you will see that love is extending its own horizon. It is identifying itself with time and, again, it is going beyond time, because it needs fulfilment. When love wants fulfilment, it will not stay with time for five or ten minutes. It will extend throughout Eternity. If you know this and meditate on your heart, then the expansion of time comes, the expansion of delight comes, the fulfilment of the soul comes. If you try to feel love, you will extend the capacity of your aspiration, extend the capacity of your realisation and extend the capacity of your oneness with the entire world.[5]

What the Heart Is Not

What we mistake for the heart is actually the emotional vital. This moment we want to give everything to a person and the next moment we want to keep everything for ourselves. This moment, for no reason, I am ready to give everything to you and the next moment, again for no reason, I am ready to take your life away. This kind of feeling does not come from the heart at all. It is the play of our demanding, unfulfilled emotions, our vital, that we are seeing.

If our vital is trying to play the role of the heart, it will try to dominate others or make them feel that they need us badly because we have wisdom or light, whereas they do not. But the very existence of the heart is based on identification. Identification is light. The spiritual heart can identify only with light and delight, for it gets continuous light and delight from the soul. We may identify with someone's sorrow, but what we are actually identifying ourselves with is the light inside that sorrow. Inside pain, inside suffering, inside darkness itself, there is light. Ultimately, the heart is identifying with the light within. If we cry every day for our own inner light, then we will see that the heart is bound to expand. But if we want to expand the heart without light, we will merely expand our ignorance. Only when we cry for the Highest will our heart really expand.[6]

The hunger of the human heart is to love and to be loved.

When the heart is hungry for love, the heart does not see in itself the light of the soul. This is because it consciously or unconsciously mixes with the vital, or we can say that the vital enters into the heart. Rather than inspire, the vital instructs or instigates the human heart to claim love from others, and the heart tries to force its way into others. This is absolutely wrong! When the human heart plays the game of possession, which is not a positive or divine quality, it finds no satisfaction because the person it possesses is a bundle of ignorance. Once again frustration and destruction play their roles. When the heart itself becomes a flood of sincerity, it sees its mistakes and feels miserable that realisation is still a far cry.

When we are insincere, we feel not only that we have reached the Goal but also that we are ready to offer the Goal to the world at large. When we are sincere, all our imperfections come to the fore and we realise how far we are from our Goal. When we pray and meditate, our heart does become sincere. When this sincerity speaks, our heart feels miserable and immediately runs to the soul, to its elder divine brother, for guidance and illumination. Then the soul guides the heart. When the heart establishes a free access to the soul, the heart is safe. The human heart at that time becomes the perfect instrument for God-manifestation on earth.[7]

Question: When you speak of the heart as being the centre of love and the place where the soul resides, do you mean the physical heart, or is 'heart' just a term you use?

Sri Chinmoy: I am not speaking of the human heart, the physical heart, which is just another organ, or the emotional heart, which is really the vital. I am speaking of the pure heart, the spiritual heart. According to my own realisation, the spiritual heart is located in the centre of the chest, in the centre of our existence.

The heart is like the commander-in-chief, while the soul is the king. When the soul comes into existence, its first concern is to illumine the heart. When the soul withdraws from the body, automatically the commander-in-chief loses all his power. The heart wants to stay with its king. It does not want to go and join another king or another army. In the outer world our friends may deceive us; but in the case of the soul and the heart, their intimacy is thicker than the thickest. The physical sometimes does not listen to the soul. The mind and the vital may ignore it. But the heart is always faithful to the soul.[8]

Meditation, the Heart and the Cultivation of Good Qualities

I hope all of you meditate regularly.* Even if you do not get immediate results, please do not be disheartened or discouraged. To pass our school examinations, we have to study for years. But meditation is the examination of our body, vital, mind, heart and soul. When we pass this examination we have learned everything, whereas for the school examination we need only limited knowledge. For the vast inner knowledge we have to study. Our study is our sincere prayer and meditation. Sincerity plays a great part. If we meditate with intense sincerity even for five minutes, that is better than sitting in so-called meditation for two hours and thinking of our children, our friends, our enemies, our jobs and what not.[9]

A beginner at meditation has to feel that he is a child, no matter how old he is in earthly age. A child's mind is not developed. When he is twelve or thirteen his mind starts functioning on an intellectual level, but before that he is all heart.

*Editor's Note: See *Meditation*, by Sri Chinmoy, for a comprehensive review of the practice of meditation, from advice on starting to expanding advanced practice.

4

Whatever he sees, he feels is his own. He identifies spontaneously. This is what the heart does. When you feel that you
are a child, immediately feel that you are standing in a flower
garden. This flower garden is your heart. A child can play in a
garden for hours. He will go from this flower to that flower,
but he will not leave the garden, because he will get joy from
the beauty and fragrance of each flower. Inside you is the
garden, and you can stay within it for as long as you want. In
this way you can meditate on the heart.[10]

If you can stay in your heart even for five minutes, even if you
do not pray or meditate, your consciousness will be raised.
There is no need to pray to the Supreme to give you this, that,
or anything else, for you will get all the things that you want
and infinitely more from the heart. But you will get them in
the way the Supreme wants to give them. If you can please the
Supreme by staying always inside your heart, you will see that
your desires are fulfilled most luminously. They may be the
same desires you have always had, but they will be touched,
on a very high level, with luminosity. Before they are fulfilled,
the Supreme will transform each desire into aspiration with
His Light.[11]

Aspiration comes directly from the heart. The heart can give
you everything. Aspiration is the harbinger of realisation or
illumination. In aspiration is the seed of realisation. Aspiration
comes from the heart because the illumination of the soul is
always there. And when you meditate on the heart, not only do
you get aspiration, but you also get the fulfilment of that aspiration: the soul's infinite peace, light and bliss.[12]

If you can concentrate on the tip of your finger, you can also
concentrate on your heart. As you concentrate on anything —
a picture, a candle, a flame, any material object — so also can

you concentrate on the heart. You may close your eyes or look at a wall, but all the time you are thinking of the heart as a dear friend of yours. When this thinking becomes most intense, when it absorbs your entire attention, then you have gone beyond the ordinary way of thinking and entered into concentration. You cannot look physically at your spiritual heart, but you can focus all your attention on it. Then, gradually, the power of your concentration enters into the heart and takes you completely out of the realm of the mind.[13]

Another way to meditate on the heart: Imagine a flower inside your heart. Suppose you prefer a rose. Imagine that the rose is not fully blossomed, it is still a bud. After you have meditated for two or three minutes, try to imagine that petal by petal the flower is blossoming. See and feel the flower blossoming petal by petal inside your heart. Then, after five minutes, try to feel that there is no heart at all, there is only a flower inside you called 'heart'. You do not have a heart, but only a flower. The flower has become your heart or your heart has become a flower.

After seven or eight minutes, feel that this flower-heart has covered your whole body. Your body is no longer here; from your head to your feet you can feel the fragrance of the rose. If you look at your feet, immediately you experience the fragrance of a rose. If you look at your knee, you experience the fragrance of a rose. If you look at your hand, you experience the fragrance of a rose. Everywhere the beauty, fragrance and purity of the rose have permeated your entire body.[14]

Question: Why do you tell people to stay in the heart rather than in the mind?

Sri Chinmoy: There are many reasons why I tell people to stay in the heart and not in the mind. The heart knows how to identify itself with the highest, with the farthest, with the inmost. In the case of the mind, this is not so. The mind may try to identify itself with an object, with a person, with something limited. But this identification is not pure or complete. But when the heart wants to identify itself with something or someone, it uses the feeling of love and oneness. When the heart wants to see something, it sees it unreservedly.

The heart expands. The soul represents our illumination, and it is inside the heart that the soul abides. In the spiritual life our treasure is the soul. It is only with the help of the soul that we can make the fastest progress in the inner life, and we can contact the soul only by meditating on our heart. All paths lead to the goal, but there is a particular road that will lead us there faster than the other roads. That road is the heart. It is faster, safer and surer than any other road.[15]

Question: Can we use mantras to cultivate good qualities? And if we can, do the mantras have to be Sanskrit mantras, or can they be in English or another language?

Sri Chinmoy: When I think of Keats' poem that begins, "A thing of beauty is a joy forever," for me it is like a mantra. You have only to repeat the line soulfully. There are many, many English phrases like this. It is only your feeling when you utter the word that matters. For me, there is no difference if I say 'purity, purity', or if I say the words *pavitrata* or *pavita*. I tell you, if I say soulfully 'purity', it is enough. We Indians are only rogues if we beat our drums and say we alone have mantras.

Whichever quality you need — courage or purity or faith, you can just repeat the English word, if you cannot formulate a line. Only repeat the word. What else is a mantra? It is a matter of repetition, repetition. Mantras can be one single word, two words or three words, or one line or two lines. But your soulfulness is of paramount importance. If you have soulfulness inside you, then you will have a perfect mantric utterance. [16]

Varied Views of the Heart

The heart awakens
All our sleeping divine qualities.[17]

An aspiring heart has the capacity
*   To enhance the quality*
Of each blossoming moment.[18]

Only when I look
*   Inside others' hearts*
Do I see my own perfection
And the perfection that I want
*   To see in them.*[19]

While walking along
The avenue of my aspiration-heart,
*   What do I do?*
I harvest my heart's sunlight.
*   How?*
Slowly, steadily and selflessly.[20]

How to Open and Expand the Heart

Each soulful thought
  In my mind
Adds to the beauty and purity
  Of my heart's glistening chandelier.[21]

We can learn to always listen to our heart if we can consciously make ourselves feel that what we have and what we are is only the heart. And what is the heart? The heart is love, the heart is oneness. If we know that the heart is the only thing that we have and that we are, then all the good qualities of the heart become part and parcel of our reality-life.[22]

There are two simple ways to open the heart. One way is to cry inwardly with utmost intensity, like a child crying for a doll. Inside your heart is your real Reality, your Beloved Supreme. If you can cry for your Beloved Supreme the way a child cries for a doll, then you are bound to open your heart's door. This is one way.

The other way is to be cheerful in every aspect of your life. If you can be cheerful no matter what happens, no matter what circumstances you are in, then you will be able to open your heart's door. A lack of cheerfulness immediately closes your heart's door. If you are sincerely cheerful, then your heart's door will remain wide open.[23]

There are also three ways in which you can become your heart. The first way is to feel that you have spread a net, in which the entire world is caught. You have caught everyone, not to punish them, not to hurt them, but to play with them. You will give them joy and they will give you joy. When you think of playing a game, you become the heart. The heart is joy, play is

9

joy, the game is joy and the player is joy. When you think of playing a game you become the heart.

The second way to become the heart is to feel that inside you there is a divine Child and that is the soul. You can constantly think that inside your heart is a Child who is most luminous, infinitely more beautiful than any human being. The eternal Child needs an abode, a house, a room. Where is His room? It is inside your heart.

The third way to feel that you are the heart is to constantly feel your need and God's need. Your need is perfection. If you can think of perfection, meditate on perfection, cry for perfection, then your need will be fulfilled. God's need is manifestation. In spite of your imperfection He is manifesting Himself, but when He can manifest in and through your perfection, then He will have real fulfilment. When God is fulfilling Himself in and through you, that is your real fulfilment and His real fulfilment. At that time you are nothing else but the heart.[24]

Question: How can we increase the power of the heart?

Sri Chinmoy: By self-giving and by being sincere in our inner cry. The more sincere we are in our inner cry, the sooner our heart-power increases. Sincerity is the living force, the quintessence, of everything divine in us. It is the motivating force that increases the heart-power in us. When we cry sincerely and soulfully, the right cause will present itself. Then we will throw our entire existence into this cause. We will give it all our aspiration-power and dedication-power. At that time, we will find that the power of the heart increases immensely.[25]

Chapter 1

HUMILITY

What Is Humility?

True humility
Is an elephant-strength
That likes to walk lightly.[26]

True humility means that we can become one with the consciousness of anything or of anyone. If we are humble, then the other person will immediately open his heart's door so that we can enter into his heart and he can enter into ours. If we are humble, the whole world will open its heart to us, because the world feels that we have the willingness or receptivity to hold it within our own heart, even though it has countless undivine qualities. In divine humility, we can see a true determination which is founded on simplicity, sincerity and purity.[27]

How can we get satisfaction from life? Satisfaction we can get only when we give to somebody else, to our larger self, to humanity. We can get joy only by becoming one with humanity, by sharing our reality with others. When we are becoming one, the whole world becomes grateful to us. So if we are humble, if we become like the tree-reality which constantly bears fruit, then only we are getting and giving satisfaction to the Supreme in mankind.[28]

A tree is humble from the root right up to the top. When we identify with a tree, we get humility. The tree protects people against rain and against bright sun. When the tree bears many fruits, it bows down with these fruits and offers them to the world at large. The tree could have been very proud, very haughty; it could have lifted its branches still higher, because it had achieved something great. But no!

When we really have something to offer, and when we want to offer it with a devoted quality, then humility automatically comes to the fore. When someone does not have anything to offer, then we say, "Naturally he has to be humble." But it is not so. The very fact that he does not have anything, that he does not have any good quality, means that it is impossible for him to cultivate humility. If he has no ordinary good qualities, how can he have the best, the most precious quality among all the divine qualities, which is humility? When somebody is really good, from him we can expect something. If he has some good qualities, then he can grow more good qualities.

First, we have to try to grow more divine qualities. It is from one good quality that we get two or three more good qualities. We have to give more importance to the divine qualities than to the undivine qualities. Gradually, the divine qualities will conquer the undivine qualities in us, such as arrogance and stubbornness. And the more divine qualities we develop within, the sooner we will have the best, the absolutely most essential quality, which is humility.[29]

Humility does not mean taking a back seat. When you take a back seat consciously and deliberately in order to show others how humble you are, you are not being humble at all. Again, if you know that somebody is superior to you, and if for this reason you sit behind him rather than in front of him or beside him, this is not actually the heart's humility either. This is only a recognition of the fact that if you are inferior to someone, naturally he deserves to be in front of you. It is his due.

True humility is something totally different: it is the feeling of oneness. Humility means giving joy to others. If you have not established or cannot establish your inner oneness with others, then at least you can try to make them feel that they are as important as you, if not more so. On the outer plane if you can make people feel that they are really important, then they will value you. Here on earth we want to get joy. But how do we get joy? We get joy not by coming forward before others, but by bringing others to the fore. The real joy we get by self-giving, not by possessing or by showing our own supremacy. When we allow others to get joy first, then we feel that our joy is more complete, more perfect, more divine. By making others feel that they are either equally important or more important, we will show our true humility. Offering joy to others first is the way to show true humility.[30]

How can you know whether it is true humility or false humility? When it is true humility, you will get tremendous joy and you will feel that the person to whom you are bowing down is in no way superior to you. It is only that you see the Supreme in him. That is why you are bowing down to him.

When you are offering insincere humility, your mind will be cursing you because it is all false. The mind will not get any joy and the vital will mock at you saying, "What kind of humility are you showing?" But when it is true humility, the physical, vital, mind, heart and soul all will participate in your action. And at that time you get tremendous joy. When you get real joy, it is true humility. When you are getting no joy or you are criticised by your own inner being or the members of your family, the vital, the mind and the physical, then you can rest assured that it is false humility.[31]

What Humility Is Not

Every day
I beg God for superiority.
He gives me humility instead.[32]

By outer means, by outer behavior, by courtesy, one can never become humble. Humility comes directly from the soul's light. When the soul's light is expressed in the soul's way by the physical being, on the strength of absolute oneness with all human beings, this is divine humility. Nothing can enter an individual so silently and at the same time so convincingly as humility.[33]

My humility does not mean that I want the world to ignore me. That is no humility. My humility wants that I should neither veil my ignorance nor make a parade of my knowledge. To be violently dissatisfied with oneself and curse one's fate is not the sign of humility. The true signs of humility are one's constant aspiration and one's inner cry for more peace, light and bliss.[34]

When we meditate, the first thing we have to know is whether or not we are humble in our inner, spiritual life and in our outer life. One who has an inferiority complex can never be really humble, but can only have false modesty or false humility. Inside, his heart is burning with jealousy, and he is all the time thinking of how to become equal to his superior and then surpass him, or how to belittle or destroy the good qualities of the superior. It is on very rare occasions that the inferior shows real humility toward the superior.

In the ordinary life, the superior person does not have humility either; he is always bloated with pride. He is stronger and he is more powerful. But one who is really powerful spiritually is humble because he knows that the ones who are inferior are also part and parcel of himself.[35]

When we see a man of determined will, we feel that he has no humility, that he is arrogant, egotistic, autocratic, self-asserting and so forth. We feel that humility and determination are poles apart. But this is because we do not understand the meaning of humility. When we use the term 'humility', we often feel that somebody has been humiliated by someone else. But humility is the feeling of sweetest oneness. It has nothing to do with humiliation. Humiliation means that somebody is trampling on us and looking down upon us; but true humility means that we can become one with the consciousness of anything or of anyone.[36]

Humility does not mean that we will be always silent and shy, when inside we are criticising others' wrong actions and wrong judgements. Humility is the true inner wealth that unites us consciously with God. When we show humility to God, He feels that we really have some inner wisdom.[37]

By feeling unworthy we will not be able to draw God's Compassion. It is absurd. Not even one drop more of God's Compassion will rain down on earth if we feel that we are unworthy. Far from it. But if we are humble, if we aspire and feel that the little capacity that we have has come from God, then we can fulfil ourselves and God will be pleased. So never feel unworthy. Only feel the necessity of real humility in your life so that God can act in and through you on your own level.[38]

There is a great difference between humility and unworthiness. Let us deal first with unworthiness. When we are about to do something, certain incapacities that we are born with may make us feel unworthy. Again, unworthiness may come as a result of something undivine that we have done. But whatever the reason, he who feels unworthy of something will automatically remain far away from the world of delight.

The more an individual has to offer to the world, the more he feels that he has to come down to the world's level. If he remains above, then he cannot be approached. God has everything to offer us: peace, light, bliss and all divine qualities. He is all Love. When He wants to offer us His Love, He has to come down to our level. Here also, when we bend, it is not that we are offering our obeisance or our surrender to someone. It is only that we have to come down to the level of other individuals in order to become one with them. When we are humble, we become totally one with the standard of the people around us. It is not through humiliation, but through illumination, meditation, concern and divinely fulfilling compassion that we come down to their level. God does it and spiritual people also do it, because that is the only way to be inseparably one with others on their own level.[39]

The Humility Road to Harmony

If you speak
From the humility-podium
   Then sooner than the soonest
You will conquer the heart
      Of mankind.[40]

There are many ways to love God the creation, but humility is of paramount importance. If we have humility, then nothing is beneath our dignity; there is nothing that we shall not do for our expanded selves.[41]

Inwardly God has made us one with Him and with His creation. Outwardly also He wants us to realise everything as one, and for that, what is necessary is the soul's light. The soul's light can be expressed only through humility, for humility has the inner capacity to identify itself with anything or anybody as its very own.[42]

Question: How can we work more harmoniously with others?

Sri Chinmoy: To keep harmony when you are dealing with other individuals, do not use your justice-light. Forget about justice! There is no justice on earth. Only think of wisdom-light. Always be as humble as possible. Even if you feel that others are idiots, use absolute humility — if necessary, use forced humility. Force yourself to be at the other person's feet, not on the other person's head. Let them increase their stupidity. Let their ego-balloon become large, larger and largest. One day it will burst. True, by becoming humble, you are pumping them up. But at least you are not increasing the disharmony. It is not something that you have to do all your life. For one or two months or a few years you will do it. Then you will see that eventually his ego-balloon will burst and he will be on the same level as you are. Otherwise, without humility, there is no way we can have harmony. [43]

Varied Views of Humility

   Ego is a cruel thief;
So is my earthly anxiety.
   Purity is a self-giving saint;
So is my heavenly humility.[44]

God forgot my name because I was disproportionately proud.
God gave me not only His Name but also His God-capacities
because I was sincerely humble.[45]

The seed of humility is exceptionally fertile. It may not germinate plants of power and force, but it does yield flowers of sweetness, grace, modesty and light.

Love for the Divine is in its essence a spontaneous spiritual humility.

Humility has no need to sit on the King's throne. But the King cannot help bringing the throne to humility. And now who is the King? God's Compassion.

A prayer, in its simplest and most effective definition, is humility, climbing the sky of an all-fulfilling Delight.

Only the true sense of humility can raise us from our knees as high as we aspire.

We must realise that there is only one way of acquiring infinite future possibilities. That way lies in the great power: Humility.[46]

Humility and Other Qualities

Certainty

There are a few things in life that have the speed but do not embody certainty. But when it comes to humility, humility has both speed and also assurance. Humility carries the speed and assurance for us to arrive at God's Palace sooner than at once. [47]

Courage

Courage challenges the world. Humility illumines the world. Courage strongly urges us to stand up for our own rights. Humility soulfully inspires us to stand up for God's rights alone.

Courage is not aggression. Aggression is man's destruction-force. Humility is not humiliation. Humiliation is man's rejection-force. Courage is man's self-determination. Humility is man's oneness-distribution. Self-determination eventually succeeds. Oneness-distribution constantly proceeds. Courage is man's conquering force. Humility is man's unifying force. Courage feeds the divine human in us. Humility feeds the unifying and immortal divine in us.

The seeker in us uses courage to conquer the teeming doubts in the mental world. The seeker in us uses humility to constantly gain faith, to increase faith in God's universal Oneness and Light.

Courage is the struggle, birthless and deathless, between man's victory and defeat, between man's joy and sorrow, between man's smiles and tears, between man's acceptance and rejection, between what man has and what man is. What man has is sound-satisfaction and what man is is silence-perfection.

Humility is man's divine and supreme glory-bird that flies from God's Infinity-Dawn to God's Eternity-Day and from God's Eternity-Day to God's Infinity-Dawn.

With courage we manifest God in our own way. With humility, God manifests Himself in and through us in His own Way.[48]

Dignity

From the spiritual point of view, in divine humility alone can true dignity abide. Human dignity, if it is not purified, is all pride, ego and vanity. It is through false human dignity that we are constantly separating ourselves from the world. But when we have divine dignity, we say, "I am God's child. I am in everything and with everything; I have to be in the world's suffering and in the world's delight." At that time we can never separate ourselves from the world or from reality.[49]

Power

Soulful humility itself is a form of divine power. There is

no difference between divine power and soulful humility. Real divine power is an aspect of the highest transcendental Power. The Mother-power, the divine power, the power of the Supreme Mother, also has its soulful humility. You cannot separate soulful humility from power. So if you just develop soulful humility, automatically you will cultivate divine power within yourself.[50]

Self-Confidence

There is no difference between true humility and divine self-confidence. What is true humility? True humility is the constant awareness of what the highest part is and what the lowest part is.[51]

Self-Transcendence

There are quite a few ways to transcend ourselves, but the two main ways are the humility-way and the awareness-way. We try to cultivate humility, true and soulful humility. It is through humility that we acquire the power of receptivity. When we have the power of receptivity, at that time peace, light and bliss in boundless measure descend from above, and with no difficulty we can embody these divine attributes.[52]

Strength

From the inner, psychic point of view, real humility and real strength go together. When one has real humility, one can have the soul's strength. At the same time, real humility comes directly from the soul, and it actually is the soul's strength. From the spiritual point of view, what we call in Heaven 'humility', we call on earth 'strength'.

When the soul's strength wants to manifest in humanity, it does so through humility. If another force is used, people will not accept the power or light or delight or peace that is offered. But people will accept something when it is given to them with utmost humility. That is why the soul finds it extremely easy, in comparison, to inject human beings with humility. When one really possesses peace, light and bliss, he becomes humble.[53]

Cultivating Humility

Humility can be achieved very fast.
Humility can be made very vast.
Humility can give us
What nothing else can give us:
Inseparable oneness
  With God's Delight.[54]

My humility is supported by two significant members of my inner family: softness and tenderness.[55]

Because of my sincere incapacity, humility, and its closest friend, divinity, have become my intimate friends.[56]

While we are constantly achieving something, we have to remember to be humble in order to be of greater service to mankind. But first we have to know that if we want to become humble, it is certainly because we want to become happy. And in self-giving we become really happy. Real humility is the expansion of our consciousness and our service. Let us always try to develop these good qualities within us and then humility is bound to come.[57]

If you know someone who is sincerely humble, then try to think of that person from time to time to increase your humility. If you increase your humility, you will be able to make the fastest progress. Humility is absolutely necessary for everybody.[58]

There is another practical way to achieve humility in the outer life. If you are a good singer and you are bloated with pride at your achievement, what you have to do is think of the world's best singer. Immediately your own achievement will pale into insignificance because this other singer is undoubtedly far better than you. Pride comes when you feel that you are in some way superior to other people or that you have something which they do not have at all. But if you will compare your capacity or your achievement with that of someone who has it in far greater measure, then your pride will have to fade. When pride diminishes and disappears, humility increases and looms large.[59]

If we take the positive approach to humility, then we feel always that we have come from God. God has created us. We are God's children. Some of us are conscious children, some are unconscious. If we have entered into the spiritual life, that means we are conscious of God's Presence. It need not be for twenty-four hours a day, but at least for one fleeting second we are conscious of God's Presence. We may not see God face-to-face, but His inner Presence compels us to meditate on Him. If our Source is God and He has created us, then we must not feel unworthy of Him. Only we should be humble, because it is through humility that God's Light can be seen, felt and manifested.[60]

You can become truly humble only by discovering, by feeling and by knowing what true humility is. True humility is conscious awareness of the transcendental and universal Reality. True humility is God's supreme Nature manifested on earth in mankind and for mankind. Of all God's qualities, humility has no parallel.[61]

In the spiritual life, the easiest way to conquer ego is to offer gratitude to God for five minutes daily. If you cannot offer gratitude for five minutes, then offer it for one minute. Then you will feel that inside you a sweet, fragrant and beautiful flower is growing. That is the flower of humility. When you offer Him your gratitude, God gives you something most beautiful, which is humility. When you discover the flower of humility inside you, you will feel that your consciousness has covered the length and breadth of the universe. In the spiritual life we grow humility through conscious gratitude. Once it has seen the flower of humility, the ego goes away because it feels it can become something better: the universal oneness.[62]

God is my superior, my only superior. I am humble to Him. This is my supreme duty. God's children are my equals. I am humble to them. This is my greatest necessity. Pride is my inferior. I am humble to pride. This is my surest safety. My humility is not self-denial. My humility in silence affirms what I truly have in my world without and what I surely am in my world within.

My humility is not the abstinence from self-love. I love myself. I really do. I love myself because in me the highest Divinity proudly breathes.

Self-conceit tells me that I can easily destroy the world. Self-exploit tells me that the world is at my feet. My humility tells me that I have neither the capacity nor the desire to destroy the world. My humility tells me that the world and I do have the real capacity and the sincere desire to cry for perfect perfection. My humility further tells me that the world is not at my feet, far from it. I carry the world devotedly towards its self-realisation. The world carries me lovingly and openly towards my self-manifestation.

When I am all humility, I neither underestimate nor overestimate my life. What I do is to judge my life exactly the way my Lord Supreme judges my life.[63]

Question: How can I achieve humility?

Sri Chinmoy: In our human life, when we have something, immediately pride, vanity and many other undivine forces enter into us. We extol ourselves to the skies. But if we can become one with the consciousness of a tree, we will feel that the more we have to offer, the more humility we will have.

Whenever we aspire we get an iota of peace, light and bliss. When we practise concentration and meditation regularly and devotedly we get abundant peace, light and bliss. When we get these qualities in abundant measure, automatically we feel that it is our bounden duty to become inseparably one with the rest of the world. The higher we go, the more we feel our universal oneness. At that time, real humility dawns. The deeper we go, the sooner we see the root. Once we become part and parcel of the root, we cannot be proud. We see that it is from the root that the trunk, the branches, the leaves, the flowers and the fruits have come into existence, yet the root mingles humbly with the earth and clay.

If you want to develop more humility, I wish to tell you to dive deep within or climb up high, higher, highest, on the strength of your inner cry. Your inner cry will lift you up into the freedom of the vast and make you inseparably one with the rest of the world. When you reach the Highest, automatically your divine oneness makes you humble.[64]

The Humility Road to God

Humility is the conscious expansion
  Of our vastness.
On the strength of our inner oneness
With God's entire creation
  We use our humility-light.[65]

It is through humility that we can dive the deepest and climb
the highest in our meditation. The easiest way to enter into the
universal Consciousness during our day-to-day activities is
through humility. When we show humility, we immediately
enter into the universal Consciousness, which is all-humility.
In humility is oneness, and in oneness is our divine Reality.[66]

When we have true humility, not false humility, God blesses us
with a new name: luminosity. When we have luminosity as our
true name, God blesses us with His Infinity, Eternity and
Immortality. Humility is the secret key to open up God's
Heart-Door.[67]

With His infinite Light, God has become one with finite and
insignificant creatures like us. The Infinite has entered into us.
We are learning from God how the Infinite can show His
feeling of oneness by identifying Himself with something inferior, something limited. Similarly, one person notices that God
is within him. That ordinary human being sees that he is superior to someone else, just by one inch, or just for a fleeting
second. Again, that other insignificant creature is superior to
somebody else, who is one inch inferior to him. So these
people should realise that they also can be humble to their
inferiors. The more we identify ourselves with the ones who
are a little undeveloped or awkward, or who are not in the

25

same fortunate position as we are, the quicker we help mankind to reach the Highest.[68]

In our spiritual life, in our life of aspiration and in our life of dedication, humility is the root, divinity is the tree and Immortality is the fruit. Only when I am soulfully humble does God allow me to make a perfect estimate of His universal Reality, His transcendental Reality and my own life. The perfect man is he whose inner being is flooded with humility. And it is he who eventually becomes God's transcendental Choice and God's universal Voice.

Humility and self-conceit are two real strangers to each other. Humility and God-awareness are two eternal friends. Humility and divinity's Reality-expansion are eternally inseparable, inseparably one.

When I am humble to my inferiors, they adore me. When I am humble to my equals, they love me. When I am humble to my superiors, they appreciate me. When I am humble to God, He claims me as His best instrument on earth. To climb up God's Vision-tree I need only one thing: humility's beauty. To climb down God's Reality-tree I need only one thing: humility's magnanimity.

There are many roads that lead to God. There is one road which is undoubtedly by far the shortest and, at the same time, most illumining and that road is the humility-road.[69]

Chapter Two

POSITIVITY

Positive Thoughts

Each good thought
Is
A new vision-pathfinder.[70]

Positive thoughts are needed at every moment of your existence in order to destroy your negative thoughts. Then, when the flame of aspiration climbs high, higher, highest, you will see that you possess a purifying fire that will burn away all your negative thoughts. From now on try to climb high and dive deep into your inner being and from there bring your adamantine will-power to the fore. Once you attack your negative thoughts with your inner will, the will of the soul, all negative and destructive thoughts can easily be annihilated.[71]

Each thought that you have is like a tiny drop in either the ocean of darkness or the ocean of light. If it is an aspiring thought, it is trying to feed you with affection, sweetness and love. If it is a desire-filled thought, it is only trying to bind you, blind you, capture you and devour you. You have to use your wisdom, which is found inside the heart. If you do not have wisdom, then at least use your intelligence, which is inside the mind. Each time a thought comes, observe it with your wisdom or intelligence. Ask yourself, "Is this thought going to bind me or make me free? Does this thought embody purity, humility, sweetness, affection, concern and sympathy, or does it embody all the negative qualities? Is this thought going to help me make progress or stop me from making progress?"

The answer has to come directly from you.

Once you decide whether a thought is a good thought or a bad thought, then you have to act. If you see that a thought is good and aspiring, if you see that it is trying to feed you with affection, sweetness and love, then follow it. Good thoughts are like a boat. If you get into this boat, it will carry you down the river of all your good qualities to the ocean of light. But if you see that a particular thought is bad, that it is filled with desire and it is only trying to capture you and devour you, then do not follow it. Just discard it.

If you can save yourself from wrong thoughts, if you can follow only your good thoughts and immediately discard all your bad thoughts, then everything that happens in your life will be positive, constructive, illumining and fulfilling.[72]

We must cherish positive thoughts, positive ideas, positive ideals. Only then will our goal no longer remain a far cry. Each man has to feel, "I am at the Feet of God, my own Master. I am in the Hands of God, my own Creator. I am in the Heart of God, my only Beloved."[73]

Question: Some people believe that you can will something to go better by just saying that good things are coming.

Sri Chinmoy: Positive thinking is good. When you are going through all kinds of negative experiences, at that time think positively.[74]

Question: How can we detach ourselves from emotions and still have feelings?

Sri Chinmoy: Why do you have to detach yourself from something that is good? If you touch a flower that is beautiful and fragrant, it gives you so much joy. Why do you have to be detached from that feeling? If you look at the sun or the moon and feel inspired, why do you have to detach yourself from that feeling? It is not good to be like a rock. If you develop the consciousness of hard stone, then you will not have any sympathy for other people's suffering.

So you do not have to be detached from the things that are encouraging you and inspiring you. Only be detached from the things inside you that are not aspiring, from the things that are binding you. But do not try to detach yourself from things that are sweet, affectionate, loving and illumining.[75]

Other Positive Forces

Anything positive
Will finally outlast
Anything negative.
Positivity is a God-made ocean;
Negativity is a man-made wave.[76]

The philosophy for the New Millennium is: do not see faults in anybody's life; do not see the faults in your own life. Only force yourself to see all the good things you have done, all the good things you are planning to do and all the good things that others have done. Now, the goal of philosophy will be only to see the light in oneself and the light in others. Then only will you be able to expedite the arrival of world-peace and world-oneness.[77]

We believe in the positive approach. From beauty we will try to get more beauty. From purity we will try to get more purity. From divinity we will try to get more divinity. If we take this approach, our bad qualities will eventually come to feel that they are not being appreciated and will go away. In the beginning it may be painful for us to separate our good qualities from our bad qualities. But if we walk only towards our goal, gradually all the wrong qualities or the burdens that we have been carrying will drop off, because those heavy loads do not care for the destination that we have in mind.[78]

Optimism keeps the seeker alive in God's Heart. Something more: God also remains alive if there is optimism in the seeker's heart. If there is optimism, there is hope. Optimism means the positive aspect of life. Optimism is always positive, positive, positive. If we have optimism, then God is alive inside our heart. And if God has optimism, which He has, then we are alive in God's Heart. Optimism keeps both God and the seeker alive in each other's hearts.[79]

Question: When we feel inner waves, should we silence them or intensify them?

Sri Chinmoy: If it is a positive inner wave, then intensify it, for intensification has the inner urge for manifestation. If it is a negative inner wave and you are not strong enough to transform it, then just silence it. But if you are exceptionally strong in the mental world and vital world, then transform the negative wave into a positive one. If you have great capacity, then transformation is the answer, for transformation increases satisfaction. But if you do not have great capacity, then destruction offers the second-best satisfaction.[80]

Every day, early in the morning, at least for five minutes, we have to exercise our positive thought, positive will, positive force. What do we mean by positive force? We mean that the Truth exists within us and is being realised. Then we try to feel that the Truth is already embodied. Finally we try to feel that the Truth has to be revealed and manifested in us and through us. Each aspirant has to feel that. Then there can be no negative force to disturb us or destroy our aspiration. Very often we allow the negative forces to attack us. If we do not give them the chance, then the negative forces have to remain thousands of miles away from us.

Now, there is also another process. If we constantly harbour good thoughts, divine thoughts, pure thoughts, then the negative forces cannot stay with us. If we cherish undivine thoughts, then the divine force cannot enter into us because it knows that the moment it enters into us it will be suffocated. But, unfortunately, human beings get immense pleasure in cherishing undivine thoughts. After cherishing divine thoughts for five minutes, we find it relaxing to cherish undivine thoughts.

Now, when we can recognise negative forces, that means we are already awakened. For an unaspiring person there is no such thing as either negative or positive forces. He cannot discriminate. And he has already surrendered to the dark forces which are around him most of the time: his fate.

Here is the difference between an aspiring soul and an unaspiring soul. An aspiring soul will never surrender to fate; only to his Inner Pilot, the Supreme. But an unaspiring soul will surrender to his fate. What is fate? It is only the obstruction created by limitation. This limitation has come directly from darkness and this darkness is the child of ignorance. So now let us try, all of us, early in the morning, to welcome divine thoughts, divine purity, divine light, divine truth. Then the negative thoughts, negative ideas, negative forces will not dare to enter into us. Later on, they will not even be willing to appear.[81]

Do Good

God has given you a pure heart
  To do good for yourself
  And to do good for Him.
God has given you a sure life
  To do good for
  His entire creation.[82]

My Soul

O Soul, I am your body. I am thirty-six years old today.
I wish to learn from you.
"Do good."
O Soul, I am your vital. I am nineteen years old.
I want to learn from you.
"Be good."
O Soul, I am your mind. I am sixty years old.
I need to learn from you.
"See good."
O Soul, I am your heart. I am four years old.
Please tell me the secret.
"Remain good."
O Soul, your body again.
What do you do with your boundless Love?
"I distribute my boundless Love to ever-expanding horizons."
O Soul, your vital again. What do you do with your infinite
Peace?
"I feed the teeming vasts of the past, present and future with
my infinite Peace."
O Soul, your mind again. What do you do with your Vision of
the ever-transcending Beyond?

"I feather the golden nest of my Reality's Infinitude with my Vision of the ever-transcending Beyond."
O Soul, once more your heart. Tell me your absolute secret, please.
"I live for the Supreme and for the Supreme alone.
This is my Absolute Secret."[83]

Question: Is it true that if one aspires to a higher life, to a spiritual level, then one has to totally give up ambition?

Sri Chinmoy: Not at all. But we have to know what is meant by ambition. We have to know what kind of ambition we cherish in the physical world. There is ambition like Julius Caesar's ambition: "I came, I saw, I conquered." This is the ambition of desire. There is also ambition in the vital world and in the mental world. But another form of ambition is wanting to be good, wanting to see God in everyone, wanting to serve all human beings because in them is the living presence of God. That kind of ambition we can and should cherish in the spiritual world.[84]

Question: Your powerful affirmation of the power of love replacing the love of power is the ultimate fulfilment. But if we are driven by insatiable desires, how can we move to the point of this fulfilment? What steps can we take?

Sri Chinmoy: We have to increase our good thoughts and actions and we have to decrease our bad ones. Suppose I am doing one good thing and ten bad things in a day. The following day, I shall try to do two good actions and only nine bad actions. Like this, anything that is good I will try every day to increase, and anything that is bad I will try every day to decrease. In this way, there shall come a time when from one good deed I will have become a multi-millionaire with respect to good deeds. Similarly, in terms of bad deeds, I will have become a pauper. In my thoughts and actions I will be doing only good things.

The positive approach is to try to increase all our good qualities. When our good qualities are increasing, our bad qualities are leaving us, because there is no longer any place for them. What is a good quality? A good quality is a quality with light. Right now I may have only an iota of light, but if I pray to God to increase my good qualities, gradually He will bless me with boundless, effulgent Light. Again, if every day I pray to Him soulfully, prayerfully and self-givingly to decrease my darkness, then naturally He is going to listen to that prayer also.

So, with the positive way we shall go to the highest Height, and with the negative approach, we shall eventually reach a point where there will be no more wrong thoughts or actions. At that time, what will come to us will be only positive things. If we pray to God to increase our good qualities and to decrease our undivine qualities, after a few weeks or a few months or a few years we will see that only goodness is flowing.[85]

Question: Once they have looked within, then what do your people do socially for the world?

Sri Chinmoy: When we go deep within, we feel peace, joy and love. Then, when we mix with the world, people see and feel these things in us. When you compare the feeling you get from an individual before prayer and right after prayer, you will see that right after prayer he will give you more joy. The peace, the joy, the light that a person receives from his prayer and meditation will inspire you inwardly or outwardly.

If we see a saint, immediately his face gives us inspiration. If we see a good person, his very presence gives us inspiration. Since we are all trying to be good people, each of us is offering inspiration to others. If we are with bad people, with thieves or hooligans, immediately our consciousness descends. Even when we mix with ordinary unaspiring people, our consciousness descends. But the very presence of a seeker who is aspiring to become good and to do good, will elevate our consciousness. We do not have to convert others; they are automatically transformed. After we have prayed and meditated, people see something in us. It is like a divinely contagious disease. This is just the beginning of our service to mankind.[86]

Question: I think people would say that the way in which you choose to discover yourself is not good for people because it tends to turn them inward.

Sri Chinmoy: I fully understand. The thing is that if I do not know who I am and what I stand for, how am I going to be of any use to mankind? First I have to have some inner conviction that I am of the Source, and I am for the Source. Reality is within as well as without. My highest Reality I can bring to the fore by entering deep within. If I do not do this, what can I offer to mankind, or how can I make humanity feel that I am of them and I am for them?

Real spirituality does not mean entering into the Himalayan caves and remaining closeted. Far from it! Ours is the path of acceptance. The spiritual path that we are following demands the acceptance of the outer world.

I do not ask my students to enter into a room and remain there meditating for hours. I tell them to mix with humanity and share what they have with humanity. The only thing is that inside they have to have something to share.

We are not satisfied with our own lives or the lives of others right now. We want to change the face of the world for the better. But if I have no capacity, then how can I be of service to you? And to develop capacity I have to dive deep within and establish a free access to the highest Source. I have to attain some inner peace and light and have something worthwhile to offer humanity. Only then can I become a perfect instrument of that Source and be of service to earth in the best possible way.[87]

Question: Are you sure that your philosophy of love and brotherhood can solve all the problems of the world?

Sri Chinmoy: If you have love for somebody, then you are not going to quarrel and fight with him. And if he has love for you, who will fight? It is because people do not have peace inside their hearts that they fight. If somebody inwardly feels that he is weak, he tries to cover up his weakness by showing aggression. He tries to show how strong he is.

Now, if I feel inwardly strong, I am not going to fight with you. And if you feel inwardly strong, you are not going to fight with me. If we have peace, then we have love. And if we have love, then we have peace. Then where is the question of quarrelling and fighting?

How do we get this inner peace? If we do good things, we become good citizens of the world. We can read some spiritual books or pray and meditate or serve the world in some way. If we become truly good citizens of the world, then are we going to fight? The question of fighting does not arise at all.

He who loves God is not going to fight. We pray to God to make us good human beings, to give us joy, to give us love, to give us peace. Who is going to pray to God, "God, give me the strength to destroy this person or that person?" All those who want to become good people share the same philosophy: love, love, love.[88]

The Past Is Dust

"Be happy and remain happy.
Forget about your mistakes,
Even the very last one."
So says my Lord Supreme. [89]

Question: How can I be assured of making good progress, if my past was not at all inspiring?

Sri Chinmoy: Suppose for seventeen years you smoked, drank and took drugs, but today you are no longer doing these things. You saw what was bad and cut it off, like the part of a fruit that is rotten. Now the obscurity and impurity are going away from your consciousness and again you are becoming luminous. Today you are crying for perfection. Previously you were all imperfection; now you are fifty per cent perfect and your perfection is increasing. Now you are getting solid experiences; you are growing into light. So why do you have to worry about your obscure and impure past? Only live in the immediacy of today and grow into the golden future.[90]

Question: How do you deal with guilt, if you have been brought up with the feeling that God will punish you if you do wrong?

Sri Chinmoy: In the Western world, unfortunately, the feeling of guilt is widespread. Where does the feeling of guilt come from? It comes from ignorance. First we do something wrong out of ignorance and then we have a guilty conscience because of our wrongdoing. Instead, the first thing that should come to our mind immediately is, "If I have the power to do something wrong, then God has the power to forgive me." When we have done something very bad we must not feel that there is no power in the universe to obliterate our wrong deeds. We have done something wrong, granted, but God is infinitely stronger than we are, and we should remember that He is all Compassion. Whenever we meditate we should feel that God is all Love. He is not going to punish us. With His infinite Compassion He is going to transform us. But if we cherish a feeling of guilt, God will not be able to come to our rescue.

Eventually the sincere seeker will recognise the fact that guilt comes from bondage. If we meditate daily, we are trying to be freed from our ignorance and limitations and it is this inner freedom, not the outer freedom, that will free us from guilt. We do not know how to utilise the outer freedom properly and we make mistakes because we are afraid of going deep within to secure our real inner freedom. But once we can use our inner freedom there will be a constant effulgence of light in our life. Then how can we do anything wrong?

I always say the past is dust. By thinking of it and brooding over it we cannot change the past or free ourselves from guilt. If we have done something wrong, it is past. Let us think of the immediate future and allow it to grow into the immediacy of today. Our aspiration, which wants to go forward, upward and inward, will bring the divine wealth from the immediate future and place it right in front of the door which we call the past. Then, when the past wants to come in to us, it will find that we have blocked the door. Let us not consciously cherish our mistakes. The past is dust because it has not given us realisation. But you are crying for illumination, liberation, realisation, and not just to be freed from guilt. Since that is your aim, you must run towards your Goal. Then you will see the things that do not help you towards realisation falling behind you in the race because they cannot bear the effulgence of light.

If you have a guilty conscience about anything, please discard it like an old rag. When you aspire you have to put on new clothes. Always try to be in the light and for the light and you will see that darkness in the form of guilt will have to leave you.[91]

Overcoming Undivine Forces

Alas, countless times
You are bringing thorns to the Supreme
By criticizing mercilessly
Those who are trying to give Him roses.[92]

Question: How can one best overcome negative forces?

Sri Chinmoy: One can best overcome negative forces just by becoming more aware of positive forces. If you want to conquer darkness, use your light-force. There are two rooms. One room is full of light and the other room is full of darkness. If you want to overcome anything that is negative or destructive, then you do not go to that room. You go to the one that has the positive aspects of life, that has light, peace and bliss. You go to the room that has the positive qualities. Then all these positive qualities you try to assimilate. Once you are inundated with the positive qualities, then you can enter into the room with the negative forces.

So pay no attention to the negative forces. Pay attention only to the positive forces. Let the positive forces become extremely powerful in your life; then you will be able to overcome the negative forces. But if in the beginning you start to pay attention to the negative forces, then you will be destroyed.[93]

Question: Can meditation help cure illnesses such as high blood pressure?

Sri Chinmoy: Meditation means our conscious awareness of our Source. Our Source is God, our Source is Truth, our Source is Light, our Source is Perfection. Our Source has no imperfection, no ailment. Where is this Source? This Source is deep within us. In meditation we make our mind calm and quiet. In the outer life it is almost impossible for most human beings to have peace of mind. He who does not have peace of mind is a veritable beggar; he finds no satisfaction in anything. Again, if we get peace of mind even for a fleeting second, we feel we have accomplished something significant in our lives. When the mind is tranquil, there is a constant flow of harmony. When there is harmony in the system, there can be no ailment. It is only in the world of anxiety, worry, tension and confusion that ailments can be found. When there is real harmony, the sufferings of human life come to an end.

High blood pressure, heart failure and all the diseases that we notice in God's creation are attacks from undivine forces. These undivine forces can be overcome only when we surrender to a positive force. When we meditate, we try to become a perfect channel for the positive forces. The positive forces are light, love, delight. At each moment in our life, the positive forces want to take us consciously to the Source, where there is only perfection.

If our mind is calm and quiet, if our vital is dynamic, if our body is conscious of what it is doing, then we are inside the palace of satisfaction, where there can be no disease, no suffering, no imperfection, no obstruction to our abiding peace, abiding light and abiding satisfaction. Meditation is a means; it is a way, a path. If we walk along this path, then we reach our destination, which is all-perfection.[94]

Trusting Ourselves

Do you want to show your strength?
Then prove to the world
That your own negative thoughts and ideas
  Are no match for you.[95]

When we doubt God we do not gain anything. When we doubt a spiritual Master we do not gain anything. But when we doubt ourselves, we lose everything. If we have to doubt, let us doubt God. We can doubt God every second, and He will not lose anything. On the contrary, God, with his infinite Compassion, will forgive us.

But when we doubt ourselves, our soul will not forgive us. The moment we start doubting ourselves, all our good qualities will be lost. If we have love or joy it will all be lost. Our self-doubt will destroy our inner possibilities. It is best not to doubt anybody, whether it is God or ourselves. But if we have to make a choice, if we are helpless, then let us doubt God. He will show us Compassion, but we will never be able to forgive ourselves.[96]

Question: How can we trust ourselves and our abilities?

Sri Chinmoy: If we rely on God, then whatever we receive from Him will be sufficient for us. You are saying you cannot trust yourself. This moment your mind is telling you that I am a good person. Next moment your mind says the opposite. And the moment after that, your mind will tell you, "Who am I to judge him? If he is a good person, let him be good. If he is a bad person, let him be bad. What do I gain by thinking of whether he is good or bad?"

The same thing happens with trust. This moment you trust your capacity. Next moment you do not trust it at all. All human beings suffer from trust and lack of trust.

How do we solve this problem? If we pray to God and depend on God for everything, then God gives us confidence. At that time, we do not have to worry. The confidence that we get from our reliance on God can never be taken away. If you love God, how can He deceive you? We cannot deceive our dearest ones. If you are a nice person, you will not deceive your mother or your father or your brother. Can there be anybody nicer than God? God is infinitely nicer than we are. If you trust Him, then He will never fail you. Your trust in Him, your faith in Him, will give you confidence in yourself. You will trust yourself, and you are bound to trust yourself, precisely because there is Someone who loves you infinitely more than you can ever imagine, and that Person is God. If you love Him, He will give you the capacity to trust in your activities.

When you do something good, inspiring and illumining, you have to feel that it is He who has done it in and through you, according to your capacity of receptivity. If you cannot trust God, then you will never be able to trust yourself. So trust God's Presence from now on, if possible all the time. If you cannot do it all the time, then try to trust Him for a few minutes a day. The more your faith in God increases, the stronger will be your faith and trust in yourself.[97]

Seeing the Good in Others

Think only of others'
Good, divine and self-giving qualities
To stay inside God's Heart-Garden,
Instead of your own mind-jungle.[98]

Question: How can we always see the divine qualities in others?

Sri Chinmoy: If you do not see the divine qualities in another person, you will feel that you are seeing a tiger, a snake, a panther, a bull or some other animal; you will see jealousy, doubt, fear or other negative qualities. When you see undivine qualities in others, you have to feel that these are ferocious animals. Then what will happen? Those ferocious animals will devour you. If you see a tiger in front of you, do you think the tiger will just go away? The very nature of a tiger is to devour you. If you see the undivine qualities in others, then immediately those ferocious animals will come and devour you.

On the other hand, if you see in each person a divine child, or a beautiful flower, or a burning candle symbolising the ascent of the flame of aspiration, you will be full of joy. If you see inside them somebody praying and meditating, or a most luminous, divine child, you will be full of joy. If you see the divine in a person, then your strength, inspiration and aspiration will increase. Every divine quality that you have will increase. The moment you think that you see an undivine quality in someone else, feel that your whole hand is full of ink. You are soiled. You can wash it with a good thought. But if you touch the ink again, even though you have washed your hand once, it will again become dirty and black. At a given moment, either you are thinking of God or you are thinking of Satan. At every moment the mind is either thinking of something positive and creative or of something negative and destructive. So the best thing is to see the positive things in others. If you consciously see the positive things, then the negative qualities cannot come forward.[99]

Question: Sometimes when I talk to others, my mind sees a duality. In the act of trying to see the good in others, I feel a separation. What do you recommend?

Sri Chinmoy: The difficulty is that if you try to see good in others with your mind, you will see good for only one minute. Then the next minute you will try to see bad in them as well. And even when you do see good in others, you will doubt whether you have seen good; you will not know whether what you have seen is really good or bad. You want to see goodness in your friend and you do see it. But the next moment doubt will come and make you say, "Is it really good? Perhaps I am fooling myself." But if you want to feel goodness in others, then please use your heart. The heart immediately identifies with the consciousness, with the essence of a person or thing. Our philosophy is the philosophy of identification. From identification we enter into oneness, inseparable oneness. First we identify ourselves with the Reality; then we feel that we are constantly, inseparably one with the Reality. In the case of the mind, the mind may see the Reality, but then the mind doubts the Reality.

Right now let us use the heart-room and remain in the heart-room as much as we can. And once our inner being is surcharged with light, then let us enter into the mind-room. At that time, the mind-room will be illumined. We have to illumine the mind-room, we have to illumine the vital-room, we have to illumine the physical-room. But let us do the first thing first. Let the light descend from above into the heart and from the heart into the mind.[100]

Question: There seems to be inside me a dark meanness which appears more spontaneous than my love and kindness. How can I combat this dark power?

Sri Chinmoy: How do you cure meanness? Not by thinking of meanness all the time. From now on, kindly take the positive side. Meanness is self-centred. By always thinking of night, by always looking at night, you cannot go into light; whereas if

44

you all the time consciously think of vastness, the sympathetic heart or oneness-heart, then automatically meanness disappears from you.

There are two rooms: one is the room of meanness, the other is the room of vastness. If you always remain inside the meanness-room and say — "How did I get this meanness? How am I going to combat this?" — then you are scared to death. The best thing is to take the positive side and remain in the other room, which is vastness, oneness. If you stay there for a couple of years, then your entire being will become surcharged with vastness and oneness. Then if you enter into the room of meanness, that room will be changed into vastness and oneness.

Both the rooms belong to you, but you have been staying in the dark room, which is meanness. You are trying desperately to come out of this room, but there is a subtle resistance in your life. You do not like it, but at the same time you do like it. Unconsciously you may treasure it, although consciously you do not. If you consciously treasured meanness, then the question of getting rid of it would not arise at all. But unconsciously we do quite a few things. So if you can consciously remain in the room that is vastness and oneness, there comes a time when your entire being will be surcharged with illumination-light. Then you can enter into the meanness-room, which is dark, obscure and impure, and illumine it.[101]

Question: You have suggested that we think of people's divine qualities rather than their negative ones, but I haven't been able to do this successfully.

Sri Chinmoy: I am most proud of you for your sincerity. Here is something that will help you. If people have good qualities, feel that you have those qualities more than they have, only

45

right now those qualities have not come forward or perhaps the Supreme is not utilising those divine qualities in you right now. If you do not see good qualities in your own outer life, you should feel that you have them but the time has not yet come for those qualities to come forward.

But if you feel that someone else's bad qualities are entering into you instead of their good qualities, then immediately you can use two weapons. The weapon of compassion makes you see their bad qualities as a heavy load on their shoulders. You will think, "I am running the fastest and I shall reach my goal, but see what a heavy load this poor fellow has on his shoulders! I pity him. But I have my own goal to reach, and when the time comes he will also reach his goal." In that way we can sympathise with him.

Our other weapon is to think, "I have no time to waste in contemplating all his bad qualities. My time is very precious. If I spend time thinking of this or that person, I am a fool. By thinking of them or being jealous of them I will never reach my goal. I will be running towards a new, self-created goal, which is all wrong."

We run the fastest when we do not look to this side or that side. If we let ourselves become distracted by thinking of the person who is either beside us or behind us but not at the Goal itself, we will fail to reach the Goal. We are running towards the Goal, for peace, light and bliss. Since we cannot get these things from the imperfect person we are thinking of, why should we waste our time thinking of him? Always think of the Goal and your problem will be solved. [102]

Positivity from a Lofty Viewpoint

Question: Is the conflict that we are experiencing in our times a detour or a destructive force at work?

Sri Chinmoy: It is neither a detour nor a destructive force in our fast-progressing times. In the first place, there is no such thing as destruction. In Indian philosophy, the three aspects of God are Brahma, the Creator; Vishnu, the Preserver; and Shiva, the Transformer. Very often Shiva is known as the Destroyer. But God does not destroy. Rather He transforms. Perfection can be achieved. For this perfection, we have to go deep within. We see that what takes place is an inner transformation of human ignorance and doubt. If you have doubt, the apparent destruction of this doubt is actually its transformation. Everything that does not help us to run towards our Goal will be transformed into something positive.

The root of all man's problems is ignorance. But do you destroy a man in his ignorance? No, you transform him. Negative forces try to cause the destruction of our inner possibilities. The force that comes from the inconscient level inside us will try to destroy all our inner possibilities.

When a negative force speaks from inside you, it will say, "You cannot be God's chosen child. Impossible! You have done millions of things wrong." The negative force will tell you that you cannot become the perfect instrument of God and that you cannot grow into His very image. Only these two things the negative force can tell you.

Immediately you have to tell this force, "All right, I have done millions of things wrong, but that is none of your business. I am not taking shelter from you. I am not going to be under your protection, under your wings. I am under the protection of the omniscient and omnipotent Supreme."

The positive force will immediately tell you, "Yes, you

already are an instrument, a chosen instrument of God. You are growing into the very image of God because God Himself is evolving in and through you. Unfortunately, you are not aware of it. That is why you are suffering. And poor God has to wait for your conscious awareness of who He is and who you are."

Every day you have to tell yourself, "I am evolving." At least for five minutes a day you have to exercise your positive thoughts, positive will, positive forces. You have to believe that in you the Truth is already embodied, in you the Truth will realise and reveal itself, in you and by you the Truth will be manifested. For five minutes a day everybody can do this. Then there can be no negative forces to disturb you or destroy your aspiration.[103]

Chapter 3

KINDNESS, CONCERN, SYMPATHY, COMPASSION

Sympathy
Is the flow and glow
Of goodness.[104]

The Power of Kindness (Story)

The kindness aspect of life carries us far, very far, towards our destination. How kindness can change human nature for the best!

There was a school with quite a few students. Most of the students were excellent. There was only one unfortunate boy who was not at all a good student. At the same time, he had a very bad habit: he used to steal. Quite often this boy missed class in order to steal people's money and other valuables.

Some of the boys lived in a dormitory and, from time to time, they found that their money was missing. This went on for a long time and the students became extremely frustrated. They had no idea who the actual thief was.

A brilliant idea flashed across the mind of one of the most intelligent students. On one particular day, this boy pretended to be sick and did not come to class. He was hiding in the dormitory. As fate would have it, the student who was in the habit of stealing came into the room to steal something, and he was caught red-handed. The good student immediately informed the school authorities. Word spread very quickly around the school that the thief had been caught. All the students came to know who the culprit was, and they started insulting him ruthlessly.

The teachers wanted to take the matter to the police. They said, "This boy should be punished! He should be put in jail!" The headmaster firmly told them, "No, I will not allow that. It will bring disgrace to my school. Plus, I really want to help this boy and also help the other students."

The headmaster called all the students and teachers together, including the boy who had stolen the money. He said to the students, "You people must be frank with me. I would like each one of you who has lost money to tell me how much you have lost."

One student said, "I have lost ten dollars." Others said twenty, thirty, forty and so on. The whole amount came to $300. There and then, the headmaster took out $300 from his own wallet and returned the exact amount that had been stolen to each student who had lost money.

The boy who had stolen all this money was badly humiliated. Then the headmaster said to him, "You may return to your classroom. You should complete all your courses."

The boy obeyed the headmaster and resumed his classes. But the other students continued to look down on this boy. They spoke about him behind his back and made fun of him to his face. When the headmaster heard what was going on, he was extremely sad. He told the students, "The way you are behaving is not good. We have to conquer people with our kindness. You are all my students. I will be the proudest person if you please try to develop kindness, compassion and forgiveness."

The head of the school was truly an excellent human being. Unfortunately, neither the students nor the teachers listened to him. They simply could not look upon this particular student kindly or favourably. Immediately after being caught, the boy had stopped his stealing. He was determined to live a good life, but he was taunted again and again because of his past actions.

The headmaster repeatedly pleaded with his students and

teachers, "I am begging you to please be kind to this boy. He has totally given up his stealing. All of us have weaknesses that we must conquer. Please try to find kindness, compassion and forgiveness inside your hearts."

Slowly but surely, the headmaster's pleading worked. People began treating the boy with sincere kindness and concern.

After four or five years, he completed his studies and went to work. He obtained an excellent job building houses. After he received his first paycheck, the first thing he did was to withdraw $300 in cash and go to his old school. The headmaster was still there.

With folded hands, the young man offered the money to the headmaster and said to him, "I am eternally grateful to you. You saved my life. Everyone else wanted to cast me into jail, but you did not allow them. I stole $300, which you yourself gave to the students from whom I had stolen the money. Now I am returning the $300 to you."

The headmaster began shedding tears of joy and pride. He embraced the young man and said, "My son, my kindness has been most powerfully rewarded. I am so proud of you and so grateful to you. In the future, my boy, do not steal. Never steal."

The young man replied, "I have completely stopped stealing. Never again in my life will I steal. I have turned over a new leaf, and it is all due to your kindness. I assure you, if and when I have children, my children will not be affected by what I have done. They will not be like me. I will only instil sincerity, kindness, concern and compassion into my children's hearts and lives, just as you have done to me."

Again and again the young man offered his gratitude to the headmaster, saying, "You saved my life! You saved my life!" Then the young man bowed to the headmaster very deeply once again and took his leave.

The following day, the headmaster related this particular incident to all the students. Most of the students who knew about the stealing episode had already passed their examinations and graduated.

The headmaster said, "Many years ago, somebody was not doing the right thing in this school. He stole money from so many students during the day while they were having their lessons. When he was finally caught, someone showed kindness to this boy. Most people wanted to put him in jail, but someone did not allow that to happen. The boy immediately turned over a new leaf and became very, very good and nice. I am telling you all this because I do not want you to repeat the same story.

"You must not develop the habit of stealing. At the same time, you must not develop the habit of looking down upon others. We all have weaknesses. At what point weaknesses will dominate us, we have no idea. If we become kind and compassionate to others, there is every possibility that our compassion, kindness and forgiveness will work miracles in their lives and in our lives as well."[105]

Why Be Kind, Concerned and Sympathetic?

Be kind, be all sympathy,
For each and every human being
Is forced to fight against himself.[106]

The very nature of kindness
    Is to spread.
If you are kind to others,
Today they will be kind to you,
    And tomorrow to somebody else. [107]

Kindness
Changes our fate.[108]

Sympathy
    Is an
Unconditional
Hope-bestower.[109]

Yesterday I discovered kindness in myself.
Today I see how beautiful and soulful I am.

Yesterday I discovered kindness in humanity.
Today I see how meaningful and fruitful humanity is.[110]

About Kindness, Concern and Sympathy

Softness includes affection, love, sympathy and the feeling of oneness. It is not just using polite or kind words. No! One has to be totally plastic. One has to all the time feel others' suffering as one's very own. Sympathy has to be the first and foremost thing in one's life, sympathy and the feeling of oneness.[111]

Sympathy is but a musical instrument. Each individual is fortunate and rich enough to have this instrument. But the most deplorable thing is this — that we play on this instrument only once in a blue moon.[112]

Sympathy is man's soulful self-expansion.
Sympathy is God's perfect satisfaction in man.
Sympathy does not walk along the narrow road of the human mind.
Sympathy walks only along the broad road of the divine heart.
Sympathy is a love-flower and a oneness-fruit.
Sympathy is at once man's lighthouse and man's treasure-island.
Sympathy is the revelation of God-Heart in man.[113]

What to Do about Difficult People

Unless and until you have developed
A heart inundated with compassion,
Do not sit on the seat of judgment.[114]

The spiritual life is not the life of indifference. But one has to have discrimination when dealing with the world. If you give your heart to everyone, irrespective of who the person is, then people may exploit you. If a thief wants to buy tools to steal with, and if someone with a magnanimous heart gives him the money without questioning what kind of person he is or why he wants the money, who will be partially responsible for his future thefts? The man who gives money to the thief![115]

Question: Sometimes, at meetings I lead, people are not on time, or they are restless.

Sri Chinmoy: We cannot discipline others. If we inwardly curse them, then our consciousness goes lower than the lowest. If we get angry with people who behave badly, it does not help us, and also it does not help them. Our anger is not going to transform them or give them discipline - no![116]

Question: Is it possible or necessary to like everyone?

Sri Chinmoy: You should have goodwill towards everybody, but that does not mean you should go and talk to everybody and show your sympathy and concern. If you try to do that, then you will have no time to think of your own prayer and meditation. Some people have no time to think of their inner life, and God-realisation is still a far cry for them. But they go to this side and that side to help everybody and make themselves feel that they are philanthropists. In most cases, they are only fooling themselves.

Goodwill we shall have for everybody, but we cannot mix with everybody. If I see a snake, I shall offer it my goodwill, I shall try to see God inside it, but that does not mean that I shall go and stand in front of it and be bitten. I will pray that the snake will change its nature, but to do more than that will be unwise.[117]

Question: How can we be tolerant of friends and colleagues when we see they are not perfect?

Sri Chinmoy: When you see that somebody is not perfect, your heart has to come forward and say that the person who is imperfect is also part and parcel of your life. Always we have to be very, very wise. Our friends or work associates who are weaker can be made stronger by our concern, compassion and sympathy. Otherwise, if we disregard the weaker ones, we will not be in the picture either! Who is good, who is bad? Just because I can say that one person is imperfect, I cannot say that I am perfect. Why should God tolerate me if I cannot tolerate others? [118]

Question: What should I do when a member of my choir says something nasty to me?

Sri Chinmoy: The other members are all your spiritual sisters, and you love them because you see the Supreme inside them. At this moment you are having such good thoughts about them. But since they are not perfect, the next moment one of them may say something nasty to you and hurt you. When that happens, just detach yourself from that person's undivine words or actions and try not to be affected.

You have been offering them your goodwill and pouring good thoughts into them. But in return, one of them may try to make you insecure or jealous; one of them may show her weakness. So what will you do? You will not throw that person out of your life. Only you will detach yourself from the undivine things that this person is throwing into you. You will say, "Oh, today she is unhappy. That is why she is throwing her undivine qualities into me. Tomorrow, when she is thinking well of me, I may have the same difficulty and do the same thing to her." Like this, you will show that individual sympathy because she has been attacked.

You will show that individual sympathy because she has been attacked, but you will detach yourself from her wrong actions or wrong feelings. You will detach yourself from her actions, not from her life. You will continue to be devoted to her and offer her your good qualities because she is your friend. If you offer her your good qualities, this will only increase her own good qualities. Tomorrow that same individual may use her good qualities to help you or show you all love, affection and gratitude.[119]

Cultivating Kindness, Concern and Sympathy

A soulful meditation
Can easily lengthen
The mind's compassion,
    Tolerance and sympathy-limits.[120]

It is not at all difficult to bring forward the heart's good qualities, such as sympathy and concern. We can bring forward these good qualities through our aspiration. We are aspiring for God, who undoubtedly has more Concern, Affection and all other qualities of the heart than we have. Our sincere aspiration can bring these qualities down from God.[121]

In the beginning, we can become compassionate by thinking of God, who has far more Compassion than we have. But eventually we come to realise that God is also inside our own hearts. At that time we do not have to think of God as our superior. Instead, we see that God is nothing but our own higher, more illumined, self. When we realise this, superiority and inferiority disappear into oneness, and we can claim God's infinite Compassion as our very own.[122]

We own peace only after we have totally stopped finding fault with others. We have to feel the whole world as our very own. When we observe others' mistakes, we enter into their imperfections. This does not help us in the least. Strangely enough, the deeper we plunge, the clearer it becomes to us that the imperfections of others are our own imperfections, but in different bodies and minds.

Whereas, when we think of God, His Compassion and His Divinity enlarge our inner vision of Truth. We must come, in the fullness of our spiritual realisation, to accept humanity as one family.[123]

Sorrow helps us immensely. It is apt to humble our pride. It chastens us. It opens our hearts to magnanimity and sympathy. To check our innumerable errors and make us watch ourselves and put us on the road to perfection, sorrow must necessarily exist in the world. [124]

Question: When I see other people's defects and imperfections I keep mulling them over in my critical mind.

Sri Chinmoy: If you enjoy thinking of others' imperfections, you will have an extra load to carry on your own shoulders. If you cherish the thought of their imperfections, then you are inviting and welcoming these things into your own nature. Already you have at least a little imperfection, but your load becomes even heavier if you think of the imperfections of others. If you remain neutral, if you say, "I have enough problems of my own. These are their responsibility," then automatically they will have to carry their own loads.

But if you are really generous, you can say, "Whatever little capacity I have right now, let me use to help those people." If you sincerely sympathise with them because they have these defects, immediately the power that you have to do the right thing, to do the divine thing, will go to them as an additional help to their own capacity. If you sympathise, you are doing absolutely the right thing. Sympathy is nothing but expansion of your consciousness-light.[125]

Question: How can I avoid feeling envious when someone else wins the race?

Sri Chinmoy: If I feel sad when I observe someone else winning a race, this will not help me. He has the capacity, so he will win. I do not have the capacity, so I will not win. But if I can appreciate his speed, automatically some of his capacity will enter into me. Through sincere appreciation we gain capacity.

When I see that somebody is running the fastest, I really feel that I am that person. Ask me to run with the fastest runner and I will be nowhere. But when the person runs, I get great joy because I feel that it is I who have run the fastest. If you can identify with other people's successes, instead of envying them, you will get a great deal more joy out of life. And of course, if you can identify with their defeats as well, you will learn sympathy and kindness as well as enriching your own experience.[126]

Question: How can I have compassion?

Sri Chinmoy: Before thinking of compassion, you have to think of oneness. If you feel oneness with someone, then compassion comes very, very easily. If someone is suffering or if someone does something wrong, if you feel that person's suffering as your own, then naturally you will show your sympathetic oneness. And inside that sympathetic oneness, inside your willingness to be part of that person's life, is not only compassion but all the other divine qualities.

If there is no sincere oneness, there will only be a superior feeling. But if there is a feeling of oneness, inside that oneness you will find all the good qualities. Everything that is divine, inspiring, illumining and fulfilling is bound to be there. You are saying that you want to offer your compassion, but this compassion encompasses all your good qualities: your good-will, your readiness and willingness to be of service to mankind, your self-giving. These you will be able to offer only if you have oneness with others.[127]

Compassion

There are two kinds of compassion: human compassion and divine Compassion. In human compassion we often deliber-ately and consciously overestimate our true inner feeling for somebody else. Everybody says that he is compassionate, but often there is great deception in this compassion. It is not actu-ally compassion that he is offering to the needy, but an overes-timated opinion of himself. But again, inside a human being divine Compassion can and must exist. This divine Compas-sion is spontaneous delight. In it there is no feeling of separa-tivity, no feeling that one is superior and the other is inferior. No! It is a feeling of oneness.[128]

Kindness, loving kindness, is a divine aspect of God. Kindness comes from God's Compassion. When God's Compassion operates in a sincere seeker, that sincere seeker runs towards God. Compassion is like a magnet. Here on earth we call a particular thing kindness or sympathy, but in the inner world we see that this very thing comes directly from God's Compas-sion, from the highest realm of Consciousness. So when God's Consciousness and God's Compassion reign supreme in an individual soul, then he is bound to run towards God, the destined Goal.[129]

Human compassion is the clever and secret avoidance of personal discomfort. Divine Compassion is the sincere and open acceptance of others' bondage and ignorance as one's very own.[130]

Compassion is kindness unfathomable. Once a son of the great philosopher William James went to visit his uncle, the great writer Henry James. The uncle gave his nephew three pieces of advice that he felt would be of tremendous help to him: the first important thing in life is kindness; the second important thing in life is kindness; and the third important thing in life is kindness.[131]

In the ordinary, unaspiring life, compassion is a very tricky word. We say 'compassion' when we mean to say 'attachment'. In the human world there is no compassion; it is all unconscious attachment. When people who live in the physical world say that they are showing compassion to someone because he is weak and he needs guidance, this is not true. It is only attachment, and from this attachment they expect an aggrandisement of their own ego. Consciously and deliberately, or sometimes unconsciously, they are trying to feed their ego.

In the human world, we can sympathise with someone and feel that we can become one with him because we are ignorant. I am ignorant; you are ignorant; so easily I can become one with your ignorance. But to say that we are showing compassion here is foolishness. The body cannot show compassion. The physical consciousness cannot show compassion. It is only the soul that can offer compassion to the physical, the vital and the mental. Only then do we see real compassion. At that time compassion is the only reality.

Outer compassion comes from inner illumination. If one is inwardly illumined, then automatically his illumination will take the form of compassion in the outer life. First comes inner illumination; then comes the manifestation of this inner illumination in the outer life. This is compassion. If one says that he is offering compassion before he is inwardly illumined, he is only deceiving himself. What he calls compassion is only his unconscious way of showing attachment towards the earth-consciousness.[132]

Concern, compassion, love: these are three rungs in one ladder. Compassion in the ordinary sense of the term, when it is given from one individual to another, always has a sense of separativity and inferiority. But in the spiritual life, compassion is nothing other than oneness itself. Compassion does not mean a sense of pity. Compassion is the expansion of what one eternally is.

On the physical plane, when one has concern, there is always a reciprocal feeling. We feel that we are concerned and the other person also has to show his concern. On the spiritual plane, it is a different matter. When we show concern, that means the other person has pulled us. On the human level, we feel that it is so difficult to help someone. But the supreme plan is that when we use concern-power, we see that there is already an inner magnet operating. Although we do not see this magnet, it is pulling us to go toward another person. The other person may also be unaware of it, but real, true concern is like a magnet.

So many times I have said that if there is love, then there is concern; and if there is concern, then there is compassion. It is like the seed, the plant and the flower or fruit. This moment love can play the role of the seed, and then from the seed comes the tree, which is concern. Then from the concern-tree comes the compassion-fruit, which flowers into oneness.

These qualities can also change their roles. Compassion becomes the seed, concern becomes the tree and love becomes the fruit. First there is oneness in the inner world. Then it manifests its compassion-seed in the outer world. When it becomes a tree, it serves in the form of concern. Then the concern-tree bears love-fruit. The seed, the tree and the fruit must go together to complete their evolution. Whether we call them concern, compassion and love, or the other way around, they always have to go together to make a complete whole.[133]

When we use our mind to understand the meaning of compassion, very often we are misled and we mislead others. But when we use our heart, we understand the meaning immediately, and we make others understand as well.

Compassion is God's immense and intense Concern for mankind. When we show compassion to others at the time of their need, compassion is sweet. When we receive compassion from others while we are in dire need, compassion is sweeter. And when we come to realise that it is God's Compassion that is enabling us to fulfil our promise both to Heaven and to earth, Compassion is sweetest. Our promise to Heaven is to reveal our divine qualities here on earth. Our promise to earth is to manifest all our divine capacities so that Mother Earth can utilise them for her own purposes.

We feel that if we can receive God's most illumining Compassion, then our spiritual journey will be expedited. But how are we going to receive this Compassion from above? We can easily do it if we can feel that we are like a child, a little divine child. When a human child cries, no matter where the mother is, she comes to comfort him for, by pleasing the child, she gets satisfaction. Similarly, when we soulfully cry for God's Compassion, God immediately descends with His Compassion-Power.

A child cries helplessly because he feels that without his mother's help and guidance he cannot do anything. But the spiritual child does not cry with a sense of helplessness. He feels that there is a Source, and that Source is omniscient, omnipotent and omnipresent. When we become soulful in our cry, we establish a free access to the Source. So the seeker in us, the divine child in us, cries soulfully and not helplessly.[134]

Chapter 4

LOVE/ONENESS

LOVE

Introduction

Every day
God tells me the real miracle
Is not walking on water,
But loving the heart
Of each and every human being.[135]

If there is true love, then we will never see the world as imperfect. We say that this world is imperfect, we know it as imperfect because we are not expanding ourselves. The more we can expand ourselves, the deeper will be our love. When there is love, there is no imperfection.[136]

If love means possessing someone or something then that is not real love; that is not pure love. If love means giving and becoming one with everything, with humanity and divinity, then that is real love. Real love is our total oneness with the object loved and with the Possessor of love. Who is the Possessor of love? God.[137]

No doubt, life precedes love.
But if love does not follow life faithfully, life is no better than death.
If you ever dare to fight against hatred, then there is but one weapon: Love.
When I love a man, I live within his ever-blossoming heart.

When I hate a man, he lives within my ever-torturing vital.
Like death, man's love is capable of levelling all ranks.

Love: Animal, Human and Divine

I sing because You sing.
I smile because You smile.
Because You play on the flute
I have become Your flute.
You play in the depths of my heart.
You are mine, I am Yours.
This is my sole identification.
In one Form You are my Mother and Father eternal,
And Consciousness-moon, Consciousness-sun all-pervading.[138]

Fear and doubt quite often torture human love. Cheerfulness
and confidence increase and support divine love. Human love
is nothing but incapacity. If we dive deep within human love,
then we see clearly that it is weak and impotent. Divine love is
capacity. Slowly and steadily it wins the race. A soulful heart, a
climbing heart, a glowing heart is always visible in divine
love.[139]

God loves us; therefore, He never sees us as imperfect. We do
not love the world. We do not even love ourselves. How many
times we hate ourselves when we look in the mirror early in
the morning and see that our face is so undivine! How many
times we hate ourselves when we look at our big stomach,
when we look at our ugly face, when we look at our puny
biceps and triceps. We look at our weaknesses, and then we see
how much we hate ourselves!

But if we see with God's Eye, it is not like that. If God is our
All, and if He sees His creation as perfect, we are also bound to

see His creation as perfect. When God uses His Love-Power, He sees that His creation is perfect. We also have to use love-power. Then the world becomes perfect.

This world is God's creation. If we use our divine love, then the whole world is perfect. If we see something perfect, are we worried? Do we become agitated? No! Our love-power has to spread everywhere. The way God sees us as perfect beings, we also have to see the world as perfect. We will say, "He is at that stage, and at that stage he is perfect. I am at another stage, and here I am perfect." But to say that where we are is perfect and where others are is imperfect, that only our body is perfect, only our soul is perfect — no, that we cannot do. God has made everyone in His own image. Wherever we are at this point is perfect for God. If I am here, I am perfect for God here. Others are perfect where they are.

Divine love is all-spreading. Divine love will make us feel that God is manifesting Himself in and through everyone. In your case He has attained a certain state, and in the case of somebody else He has attained another state. God is happy with what He has, and He has given to each individual His own Happiness. Because of His Love, He is happy. Our love also has to be like that. Because of our love, we can be happy with each human being.[140]

Divine love is a flowering of delight and self-giving. Human love is the gamboling of sufferings and limitations.

Love is a bird. When we encage it, we call it human love. When we allow love to fly in the all-pervading consciousness, we call it divine love.

Ordinary human love with its fears, accusations, misunder-standings, jealousies and quarrels is a fire clouding its own brightness by a pall of smoke. The same human love, arising from the meeting of two souls, is a pure and radiant flame. Instead of smoke, it emits the rays of self-surrender, sacrifice, selflessness, joy and fulfilment.

Human love is often the terrible attraction of bodies and nerves; divine love is the ever-blossoming affinity of souls. Divine love is detachment; human love is attachment. Detachment is real satisfaction; attachment is quenchless thirst.

Ascending love, arising from the soul's joy, is the smile of God. Descending love, carrying with it the passion of the senses, is the kiss of death.

Human love is usually self-embracing and self-persistent. Divine love is all-embracing and self-existent.

Love can be as brittle as glass or as strong as Eternity, depending upon whether it is founded in the vital or in the soul.

Our higher emotions, taken away from their human objects and offered to God, are turned into divine nectar by His magic. Our lower emotions, if not transmuted and transformed, are turned into poison by our own hand.

Disappointment skillfully dogs vital love. Satisfaction divinely consummates psychic love.

When our vital wants to see something, it has to look through self-love. When our psychic being wants to see something, it sees through self-giving.

Human love says to divine love: "I cannot tolerate you." Divine love says to human love: "Well, that is no reason for me to leave you."[141]

There are various types of love: animal love, human love and divine love. In animal love we see, we feel and we become the instrument of destruction. Animal love is another name for unlit, obscure, dark passion. Animal love is not human love; but if human love is not transformed or purified by the divine light, there is every possibility that it will be covered by animal love. That is because the animal is still deep inside us. Each human being has inside him animal qualities and divine qualities. At every moment, he is pulled either by the divine or the undivine. The undivine here is animal love.

With human love, we have to be extremely careful, because human love is very limited. In human love, there is every possibility of being captured by pleasure. In human love there is practically no opportunity to expand our divine consciousness. True human love, even if it is not spiritual, will have some psychic emotion in it. This emotion will try to show us that love should not bind or impose. However, in human love we always feel that the other person does not want us or need us. There is always some fear or hatred in human love. Human love ends in frustration and frustration is followed by destruction. In human love, we end up losing our own sweet feeling of oneness with the other person and we end up losing our divine reality.

Divine love makes no demand. It is spontaneous and constant. It is unlimited in every way. It is like the sun. The sun is for everybody. Everybody can use the sunlight, but if we keep our doors and windows shut, what can the sun do? It is God's divine Love that has to act in and through the human love. But if we do not care for the divine love that is flowing around us or wants to flow in us, then the divine love cannot function in and through us.

Human love binds; but before it binds it is already bound. Divine love illumines, but before it illumines, we see that it is already illumined. Divine love starts with the awareness of some higher reality. It is our constant conviction of some high, very high truth. Divine love at every moment illumines us and in illumination we see total fulfilment.

God is all Love; God and God's Love can never be separated. God is highest and most powerful because of His Love. But human love has simply killed God's divine Love. Human love has been misused to such an extent that God's divine Love has been suffocated. We are using only our human love, which is binding, and we are thinking that this is our real achievement or fulfilment. But at the end of our journey, we see that it is all frustration, all destruction.

The very nature of human love is to stick only to one person and to reject everyone else: accept and reject, accept and reject. But in divine love, which is unlimited and infinite, the question of acceptance and rejection does not arise at all. In divine love there is no possession — only a feeling of oneness. This oneness can enter into an animal, into a flower, into a tree or even into a wall. It is not like human love where today we want to possess one person or thing, tomorrow two persons, the day after tomorrow three. When we have divine love for someone, at that time there is, automatically, inseparable oneness. No bridge is required; we just become one. The lover becomes the beloved, the knower becomes the known and the seeker becomes one with the Master.

Divine love tells us that we are greater than the greatest, larger than the largest; it tells us that our life is infinitely more important than we imagine. Divine love means constant transcendence, not only of our human boundaries, but of God's own Realisation in us and through us.

Divine love will come from the spiritual Master, from God and from our own meditation, but only when we do not expect it. When we do not expect anything from God, God will give us everything. He will say, "It is I who am giving the infinite Love. How is it that My children remain with very limited capacity, very limited achievement?" So in order to prove that He and His children are one, that we are His worthy instrument or representative, He will give us of His infinite Peace, Light and Bliss. Just because we love, we are spreading our peace or power. God Himself manifests everything through love. Here on earth and there in Heaven, there is only one thing that God is proud of and that is love, divine love.[142]

Love: Detachment and Attachment

If human affection is not always reliable, it is also not always harmful. Foolish is he who thinks that affection should be turned into indifference in order that God might come to him. Alas, he has yet to learn that God is All-Affection.

Affection and attachment need not always go together. An entire rejection of all relations can never be the promising sign of progress towards realisation.

Controlled desire is good. Better is non-attachment. Best is it to feel oneself removed from the snare of nature. Suppression is as hostile and undeserving as attachment. It is our non-attachment that is the only master of nature.

Desires and hungers have one common enemy: detachment.

Detachment and not possession should be the bridge between you and the object of your love.

Spiritual detachment intensifies the seeking of our hearts, purifies the vibrations of our bodies, transforms the ignorance of our consciousness into knowledge.

Granted, loneliness is a kind of spiritual disease. But human association can never be its lasting medicine. The only permanent cure for it is inner experience.[143]

Why Love?

Love is the meaning of life.[144]

Each time I love mankind
  Unreservedly,
Each time I love God
  Unconditionally,
I reclaim a part
  Of my own real life.[145]

71

In the garden of love-light,
In silence-dream,
O Beauty Eternal,
This heart of mine
Is in Your Embrace.[146]

You must regard the persons around you as limbs of your own body. Without them you are incomplete. Each person has a role to play. You may feel they are less developed, but they also have their role to play. Your thumb is much more powerful than your little finger. But the little finger also has its job. God has given us ten fingers. Now your middle finger is the tallest. If you feel that for this reason you do not need your shorter fingers, then you are sadly mistaken. If you want to play the piano or if you want to type, then you need all ten fingers.

You can love the people around you only when you feel the necessity of real perfection. If you remain isolated as an individual, then your spiritual achievement will be limited. For it is only by accepting humanity as part and parcel of your own life, and by perfecting humanity with your own illumination, that you can perfect yourself.[147]

Question: Will it help me to love people who have hurt me, people who are really very bad?

Sri Chinmoy: You say that in this world, you feel that some people are bad, really very bad. In this world, all people are not nice. Now by feeling that a person is very bad or by hating that person, are you gaining anything? All right, you think someone is very bad. But either you will love him, or the opposite thing, you will hate him. Usually it is very difficult to be indifferent to someone when he has done something very hateful to you. Your immediate reaction will be to hate that person.

But you will see what you have gained by hating that person, whether in fact, you have gained something or lost something. That particular person has not gained anything from your hatred. But what have you done? By hating that person, you have lost something very sweet in you. You have lost something. Why should one lose something very precious of her own, just because she wants to correct someone by hating him? In this world, we have to be very wise.

You will say that he is very bad and that you have to do something. But hating is not the right instrument. If you want to use the right weapon, love will be the most effective. You may think that love is not strong enough, whereas hatred is just like a sharp knife. No. The power of love is infinitely more powerful than the power of hatred, because when you love someone, at that time his divine qualities have to come forward. Someone has done something nasty to you. Alright, but now what do you want? You want to punish him and strike him? After striking him, what will happen? In you, there is something called a conscience. That conscience will prick you. You will say, "What have I done? He has done something wrong, true, but now I have done something worse. Then in which way am I superior to him?"[148]

How Can People Have Love?

Heavenly Father,
*   Awaken my heart.*
Ignite my age-long darkness.
*   Fill my Temple of Light*
*   With Your Fragrance-Beauty.[149]*

Question: How can people have love?

Sri Chinmoy: If we do not have love, what are we aiming at?

If we do not love the world, that means we can be neutral or indifferent to the world. When we hate the world, we destroy ourselves. Again, when we are indifferent, we do not get any joy. We have to love the world and accept the world as our very own. What for? For the betterment of the world.

Your question is, how can we have love? The answer is, if we do not love, what happens? The world that we are now facing is all hatred, all supremacy. By not loving one another, we are suffering so much.

But how to love someone or something? First, if we do not love ourselves, we cannot love others. If we are happy early in the morning, then on the street whomever we see, we try to greet or give a smile. But if in the morning we are unhappy, then we do not even look at others. We feel miserable and we may even go to the length of saying that if we see others, we have ruined our whole day. If we are happy inwardly, then the whole world is good for us. But if we are miserable deep within, then we blame the whole world. We never blame ourselves; we blame the world. And who is actually at fault? It is we who are to be blamed.

So how do we love the world? I wish to say that we can love the world by creating joy. From joy we get love and from love we get joy. How do we create joy? We get it by doing something. A little child gets joy by playing with her doll. If I have faith in God, by praying to Him I get joy. When I get joy, I immediately find that I want to apply it in my day-to-day life. Then this joy is transformed into love. I wish to say that we must pay attention to the things that give us joy. Then from joy we can get love. We have to start with joy. We came into the world to give joy and to accept joy from the world. But, unfortunately, many people are using the mind instead of the heart. That is why they find it so difficult to get joy from the world. The mind's only joy is to divide and divide. By cutting the reality into pieces, the mind tries to get joy. The heart wants to keep that reality intact. It does not want to cut the reality into pieces.

So our heart is the answer. The heart has joy and the heart has love, whereas the mind is empty of joy. Something more, the mind takes away all our inner joy that we derive from the heart. Because of the mind, we doubt others, we become jealous of others. If somebody is good or if somebody has achieved something remarkable, we use the doubting mind and we try to belittle that person or the achievement of that person. By doubting somebody or by becoming jealous of someone, are we getting any joy?

If we use our heart, on the other hand, to identify ourselves with that person, we get such joy! If we are using our heart to listen to a most lovely and beautiful piece of music, we will identify ourselves with the music, with the singer or with the melody. We may even feel that we are the singer, that we are carrying the melody. But if we use the mind, then we become jealous of the singer, jealous of the music and so forth.

When we use the critical mind, who becomes the loser? We do. By criticising someone, we will never, never be happy because our inner nature is all love, abiding love. That is why, in our philosophy, we give so much importance to the heart. The heart accepts the reality as such. The heart does not mind whether others are good or bad. By offering its goodwill to others, it becomes inseparably one with them. The mind, on the other hand, constantly plies between the good qualities of others and their bad qualities. This moment it says that so-and-so is a good person; next moment it tells us that we are wasting our precious time by remaining with that person. By approaching others with a heart of goodwill, we establish a kind of friendship or oneness with their soul and this gives us tremendous joy. But if we approach others with the mind, then we will only try to find fault with that person.

The heart gives joy and the heart receives joy. The mind

tries to destroy the beauty or the reality that the mind sees. Naturally, those who are being criticised by others will respond in the same way. They will muster the strength to defend themselves. So the heart is mutual love and the mind is mutual destruction.

When goodwill works, immediately we open up our heart's door. This is how we liberate our heart. This first step, the opening of the heart, is most satisfactory. Then tomorrow we will see that many, many divine qualities are blossoming inside us. Like a flower that blossoms petal by petal, in exactly the same way many, many divine qualities in our heart will blossom and they will give us tremendous joy. And we will feel that there is great meaning in our life—that meaning is to increase our love, joy, peace and bliss on a daily basis.[150]

ONENESS

Service is love
Visible and available.
Love is oneness
Inseparable and invincible.
Oneness is perfection
Immortal and supreme.[151]

Introduction

Oneness is the only relationship that can forever last, because all human beings are either conscious or unconscious sharers of one divine and supreme Reality. If we are unconscious sharers, the body-consciousness separates us, the vital person-ality separates us, the mental individuality separates us. But for the conscious sharers, there is only psychic unity. If we are conscious sharers, the psychic unity awakens us, illumines us, fulfils us and immortalises us. The human personality is a grain of sand on the shore of Infinity. If I maintain an existence separate and different from yours, then I need you to be my supplement and my complement. Our human unity ultimately blossoms into divine oneness. If I am one with you and you are one with me, then together we will grow into the highest Reality. Together we will increase our length, depth and height. Eternity's rest will welcome us, Infinity's breath will shake hands with us, Immortality's height will embrace us.

In this world, we notice that one thing alternates with another. Day alternates with night, fear alternates with courage, doubt alternates with faith, self-love alternates with God-love. But when we become unconditionally surrendered seekers of God, our oneness with God never alternates.

With our human ego we try to establish oneness with others. We feel that we have more capacity than others, so therefore we are entitled to oneness with them. But if we try to use ego as an instrument to establish oneness, then we will never succeed. Our oneness with others entirely depends on our soulful love. If we use the reasoning mind, then we can never discover love within us. If we use the demanding vital, then we can never discover love within us. But if we use the loving, fulfilling heart, then oneness becomes a reality in our day-to-day life.

When evening sets in, the glow-worms offer their light. They feel that it is they who are illumining the entire sky. A few hours later the stars appear. Immediately the light of the glow-worms becomes insignificant, and their pride is smashed. After some time, the moon appears. When the moon appears, the stars pale into insignificance. Finally, the day dawns and the sun brilliantly illumines the whole world. The glow-worms, the stars and the moon all come to realise that it is the sun that illumines the entire world, that it is the sun that has boundless light. In the spiritual life, we eventually come to realise that there is an inner sun. This inner sun is infinitely brighter than the outer sun. When we bring to the fore this inner sun on the strength of our aspiration, we establish our inseparable oneness with the world at large.

Our sense of immortality, our sense of spirituality and our sense of an inner bond, compel us to feel the necessity of oneness. Oneness is our transcendental Light and oneness is our eternal Delight. [152]

The Soul's Oneness-Power

Develop soulfully pure tears
  Of oneness-love.
Then the universal life of beauty
  Will be all yours. [153]

The mind-power is afraid of the heart-power. It is afraid of the heart-power because it thinks that it will lose its individuality and personality the moment it enters into the vast sea of oneness of the heart. Unfortunately, the heart-power is also afraid at times of the mind-power. It feels that it will be totally destroyed in the volcano of the mind's destructive sense of separativity. But this unfortunate fear of the heart's does not last forever. The soul eventually gets the opportunity to convince the heart that its qualities — softness, sweetness, kindness, sympathy, sacrifice and feeling of divine oneness with the inner Supreme Pilot — can never be destroyed. When the aspiring heart accepts this loftiest message of the soul, the heart no longer fears the mind. On the contrary, it invites the mind — not challenges, but invites and welcomes the mind — to receive the light that it has already received from the soul.

The mind-power wears out long before it reaches its

destination. If it misuses its power, then it loses its capacity very soon, sooner than at once. Even if it properly uses it, the mind-power does not last forever. The mind-power does not house inexhaustible reality.

The heart-power, which is founded upon the oneness-power, the soul's oneness-power, is at once the expression and the revelation of the transcendental Vision and the universal Reality.[154]

Question: How can people have faith when we have so much suffering in the world?

Sri Chinmoy: How can we free ourselves from suffering? We have to first of all love others and establish the feeling of oneness with them. This oneness is based on our inner existence. When we truly sympathise with somebody, then we take away some of his suffering. Let us say somebody's mother has passed away. If you happen to be a close friend of that person and you go there to console him, then you definitely decrease his suffering. Because you are sharing the suffering, the members of the family do not suffer the full amount.

Suffering is there, but we can share it by establishing our oneness with those who are suffering. Always we have to have the feeling of goodwill. If, in your suffering, I go to be of service to you and vice versa, then we decrease the suffering.

A day will come when there will be another way of conquering suffering, and that way will be through light. Human life is composed of darkness and light. Darkness wants to envelop us and destroy light; light wants not to destroy darkness, but to illumine it. In the outer world, there will always be suffering, but there is a way to diminish the suffering and that way is the way of oneness, the establishment of oneness. If we use our sympathetic heart, our feeling of oneness, then the suffering is lessened to a considerable degree.

The ultimate goal of this Mother Earth, this earth-planet, is not suffering, it is joy. We came from Heaven, which is all joy. Now, on this particular planet, we are sad, unhappy, miserable, and for that we have to take the blame to a great extent. But consciously if we can expand and extend our love, goodwill and feeling of oneness, plus if we can go deep within, then there will be much less suffering. The ultimate goal of every human being is happiness. We know that we came from Heaven, which is nectar-happiness, and we are now passing through a longer than the longest tunnel which is dark and unlit. But we feel that at the end of the tunnel, no matter how long it is, light will again be waiting for us, and that light is happiness.[155]

Expansion of Oneness

How will you recognize Heaven?
You will recognize Heaven
With your unconditional oneness-love
For the world.[156]

Oneness has to become fulness. Oneness has to become complete and perfect, and that perfection comes only from expansion, expansion, expansion. The imagination of the mind will try to get joy by saying, "I am one with the whole world." But the mind's oneness is all theoretical. The heart will say, "Am I one with my own body, first of all? Have I established my oneness with my big toe, with my defective knee, with my back pain?" I have to know if my oneness with my whole body is perfect. If any part of my body is dislocated or defective, have I established my oneness with that part?

Again, if I notice somebody who is weaker than the weakest, I may not get joy. But oneness has to be universal, because God created both the strong man and the weak man. I have to be one with the strength of the strongest man, and again, I have to be one with the man who is weaker than the weakest.

Oneness has to spread. We have to have oneness with the little flower and with the big tree. As soon as we see a flower or fruit, it is so easy for us to have the feeling of oneness, but we may totally ignore the huge tree. We look at the flower or fruit and we are satisfied; we do not pay any attention to the tree. But who produced this little flower and fruit? It was the tree. Again, who produced the tree? It was God Himself. Some human beings have achieved so many things. But who created those human beings? Again, it was God. By expanding our feeling of oneness with the creation, we can reach God.[157]

Cultivating Oneness

Be not afraid
  Of the unfamiliar.
Be not afraid
  Of the unknown.
Just cultivate your oneness-heart-soil.
You will see that
Nothing can remain unfamiliar
And nothing can remain unknown.[158]

Cultivate concern, you will reap a harvest of love. Cultivate compassion you will reap a harvest of delight. Cultivate oneness, you will reap a harvest of God's Glory and Pride.[159]

There cannot be total oneness, constant, eternal and inseparable oneness unless and until one has established oneness with the Supreme.[160]

Where does oneness come from? From aspiration. Aspiration means the inner cry that goes up high, higher, highest. When we do not consciously aspire to go high, higher, highest, what happens? Automatically the law of gravity pulls us down. We see that those who are not aspiring are constantly staying at one level. Every day they are caught by endless desires. They are at the mercy of desire. But if you aspire, it is just the opposite. Today you have a little feeling of aspiration, a little feeling of a good quality inside you. Tomorrow, when you meditate, this good quality will increase. The day after tomorrow it will become very vast. The following day it will become infinite. When you start with one desire, the next day you have a stronger desire, and the following day the strongest desire. Each day desire is binding you, grabbing you, strangling you. But when you start with aspiration, each day aspiration frees you, liberates you, immortalises you.[161]

Question: What is the best way to develop oneness?

Sri Chinmoy: We have to go to the right place. If we want light, we go to a room that is already illumined. We do not go to a room that is unlit. Oneness is only in light. The nature of light is to spread and to unite. Darkness can also spread, but it cannot unite. It only divides. Inside the heart is light. That is why the heart enjoys only expansion. So consciously, as often as possible, when you are talking to someone, when you are reading or working, try to feel that your existence is inside your heart. You have to feel that each thought is coming directly from your heart. Each time you can feel that a thought is coming from your heart, then you will automatically feel that it is coming from the Source, which is all light, all oneness. Oneness you can develop only by having the right thought blossoming from the right place. The right place is inside the heart.[162]

Question: How can we have oneness with our fellow workers when they are behaving in unspiritual ways?

Sri Chinmoy: If your fellow workers are not spiritual or spiritually inclined, then you have to exercise more compassion and sacrifice than usual. If somebody needs more kindness and affection, then you should be ready to give it to that person — not according to what he deserves but according to your own heart's magnanimity. If somebody is nasty to you or is not helping you in your work, you have to take it as a challenge to become extra nice, extra kind and extra sweet so that you can bring forward the good qualities in that person. Some people are good, some are bad. If we treat bad ones the way they treat us, we will enter into the animal world. So we have to work in a divine way and try to conquer them through patience, concern and love.[163]

Oneness and Other Qualities

If you want to understand a thing
  Sooner than the soonest,
Then do not try to interpret it.
Just love it
And become inseparably one with it.[164]

Anger

On the human plane there are quite a few undivine forces that attack us and eventually compel us to surrender: anxiety, worries, anger, attachment and self-pity. Anger: what is it, after all? Anger is a force that does not permit us to be consciously aware of our oneness-reality with others, who are our extended, expanded reality. When anger assails us, we not only forget our oneness-reality with others, but we actually destroy our oneness-reality.[165]

Confidence

There is a great difference between human confidence and divine confidence. In human confidence there is always a feeling of superiority. I am one inch higher than you, so I can lord it over you or guide you or mould you the way I want. But divine confidence is not like that. Divine confidence is the recognition, acceptance and inner assurance of oneness. And this oneness is guided, moulded, shaped, fulfilled and immortalised by a higher reality, the highest Reality, which is the Supreme. When we have divine confidence, we feel that we are God's instruments and that God is guiding us, moulding us, shaping us. But when it is human confidence, there is no God; there is only you and I, and I am one inch higher than you; therefore I can dominate you and fulfil myself in my own way.

In divine confidence, we share our capacity, we share our necessity. I am doing my respective job, whatever is asked of me, and God is doing His job, whatever is asked of Him. So I have confidence because I know I am of Him and for Him, and He is of me and for me. And God has confidence in me because He knows that from His Silence He has created me. I am His creation. If the Creator and the creation do not become the obverse and reverse of the same reality, then the Creator will not feel satisfaction. For the creation is like God's mirror. He looks into the mirror, His own Reality, and if He does not see Himself in what He creates, then He can never be satisfied. I as an individual have to become an exact prototype of His Reality. That is what God wants.

So divine confidence is our acceptance of the divine Reality which is within us, as our very own. With divine confidence I do not compete. I do not challenge. I have become one with the reality that he has or is or represents, for I am also the same reality. Inside us there is only one Reality and that is God Himself singing the song of universal oneness and the song of constant self-transcendence.[166]

Friendship

There is human friendship and there is divine friendship. Human friendship says, "Give me, I need." Divine friendship says, "Take me, for I am all yours." The human is us has not only failed us time and again, but it will always fail the ultimate test. The divine is us has always succeeded and will always succeed when it is allowed to come forward and act in and through us. This divine success is nothing short of world-harmony and universal harmony, world-peace and universal peace, world-satisfaction and universal satisfaction. Divine friendship is founded upon oneness. The source of divine friendship, divine love and divine concern is oneness. For this reason, divine friendship is lasting.[167]

What Do We Really Want?

Oneness bravery
Means freedom from self-slavery.[168]

We want happiness and we need happiness. In this life of ours there are many things that we want but actually do not need. But when it is a matter of happiness, we not only want it, but we also need it. Right now, here on earth, we enjoy false happiness in the body, vital, mind and heart. The body enjoys happiness in the world of pleasure and lethargy. The vital enjoys happiness in the world of aggression. The mind enjoys happiness when it doubts and suspects. The heart enjoys happiness when it treasures insecurity. This is the way we enjoy happiness in the beginning. But there comes a time when real happiness, divine happiness, dawns. At that time the body is fully awake and consciously offering its service-light, the vital is dynamic, the mind is calm and quiet and the heart feels its oneness, its inseparable oneness, with the rest of the world.[169]

Man has countless desires. He thinks that by fulfilling his desires he will be able to prove himself superior to others. When his desires are not fulfilled, he curses himself; he feels that he is a failure, hopeless and helpless. But God comes to him and says, "My child, you have not failed. You are not hopeless. You are not helpless. How can you be hopeless? I am growing within you with My ever-luminous and ever-fulfilling Dream. How can you be helpless? I am inside you as infinite Power."

Then man tries to discover something else in order to prove his superiority. He tries to exercise his power violently, aggressively. He wants to prove to the world that he is important. In order to prove his eminence he adopts any means, and his conscience does not bother him. God, out of His infinite Bounty, again comes to him, and says, "This is a wrong choice. You cannot prove to the world that you are matchless, unique. What you actually crave from your superiority is joy, boundless joy. But this boundless joy will never be yours unless you know the secret of secrets. And that secret is your indivisible oneness with every human being on earth."

Then God continues. He says that He is strong, He is happy, He is fulfilled, just because He is totally one with each human being, with the entire universe. Only when one is totally united with the rest of the world can he truly be happy. And this happiness makes a man unparalleled on earth. It is not power that makes us feel that we are superior or makes us feel that we are priceless; it is our matchless oneness with God and the world. It is not because we have power that others need us. No, what others badly need is our soul's oneness. We are great, we are greater, we are greatest only when we consciously feel our oneness with the entire world.[170]

Without Love, We Cannot Become One with God

When I became a voyager of light
I gave my all to love
And love gave me
Its fountain of perpetual peace
To feed God's earth-reality
  And
Expand God's Heaven-Dream.[171]

Love is the inner bond, the inner connection, the inner link between man and God, between the finite and the Infinite. We always have to approach God through love. Without love, we cannot become one with God. If we go through our journey with absolute love, we can never fail to reach God or fulfil Him, either in our own lives or in humanity.

Love is the secret key that allows a human being to open the Door of God. Where there is love, pure love, divine love, there is fulfilment. Where there is no love, it is all misery, frustration and death. The first step in our journey is love, the second step is devotion and the third step is surrender. First we have to love God. Then we have to devote ourselves to Him alone and finally we have to be at His Feet and fulfil ourselves.

Whom are we loving? We are loving the Supreme in each individual. When we love the body, we bind ourselves; when we love the soul, we free ourselves. It is the soul in the individual, the Supreme in each human being, that we have to love. Nothing can be greater than love. God is great only because He has infinite Love. If we want to define God, we can define Him in millions of ways, but I wish to say that no definition of God can be as adequate as the definition of God as all Love. When we say 'God', if fear comes into our mind, then we are millions and billions of miles away from Him. When we repeat the name of God, if love comes to the fore, then our prayer, our concentration, our meditation, our contemplation are genuine. There can be no greater wisdom, no greater knowledge, than love. We pray to God. Why? We pray to God just because God is all Love. God is not like a schoolmaster with an iron rod who strikes us all the time. Just because God is all Love, all Compassion, we go towards Him and not towards anybody else. The supreme knowledge lies in love.

We cannot bind divine love with our human thoughts, ideas, or ideals, but we can bind divine love through constant self-sacrifice. Divine love is infinite, but we can bind the infinite in us through self-sacrifice. What is this self-sacrifice? Self-sacrifice is our constant eagerness and inner cry to be shaped only by the Highest in us, by the Inner Pilot in us. But even if we offer our heartfelt and soulful obedience to the Inner Pilot in ourselves, we have still not fulfilled our part totally. But if we can bravely and sincerely tell the Inner Pilot that it is He who will be responsible for our lives, for our realisation, and for our soul's manifestation on earth, then only will our role be totally fulfilled.

Love means acceptance. What are we going to accept? We are going to accept this world of ours which is around us and within us. If we do not accept the world, which is God's outer Body, then we are negating and denying God silently and secretly, if not categorically. After we accept the world, we have to serve the world that we have accepted. If we want to serve the world in the way that the world wants to be served, then we shall always remain in ignorance. At the same time, we will not be able to throw an iota of light on the world's inner and outer problems. We have to serve the world the way that our Inner Pilot wants us to serve. Then, we shall not only fulfil the Supreme in us, but fulfil the Supreme in the world.

We get a kind of joy when we identify ourselves with someone who is all fear. We go to help him solve his problem, and then we are caught in his fear. We go out to sympathise with others, so we suffer with them and then we cannot come out of their suffering. True, it is good to identify with others' suffering, but it is foolishness to identify with someone's problems when we cannot make him bolder or braver, when we cannot make him face the reality or help him see the divine strength in himself. What is the use of showing sympathy to someone when we cannot show him our warmest power or give him solid guidance towards the light?

How can we help our sisters and brothers of the world? We can help if we become all love for the One who is eternally all Love. Let us love the One, the root of the tree. Then we shall see that the branches, the leaves and the foliage of the tree also will feel our love. Each individual who fulfils God and His creation embodies God's living Concern and living Sacrifice. And it is in this Concern and Sacrifice that God and man are both fulfilled.[172]

Chapter 5

SELF-GIVING

What Is Self-Giving?

My life's self-giving
Is the sweetness
Born of my soul's oneness.[173]

What is self-giving? Self-giving is a supreme art. From this art I come to realise that I have to fathom my unknown realities and I have to know my higher self, which abides deep in the inmost recesses of my heart. I have to become consciously and inseparably one with my higher self, which is in perfect tune with my Beloved Supreme constantly, and I have to manifest my yet-unmanifested realities.[174]

To love somebody is to see the Supreme in him: Self-giving is the sunlit path that leads me to my transcendental Destination where the Supreme is eagerly waiting for me, for the human in me and for the divine in me. The human in me is my cry; the divine in me is my smile.[175]

Happiness is what God eternally has and what God supremely is. Happiness is not something inside the heart of self-giving. No! It is our unconditional self-giving itself. Self-giving is God-becoming, slowly in reality, steadily in divinity and unerringly in immortality.[176]

Not by establishing an empire can man achieve abiding satisfaction, but only by self-awakening and self-giving.[177]

In self-giving you offer your all, whereas in charity you just give a portion of what you have and feel that it is more than enough. Total self-giving is found in the spiritual life when you have the capacity to identify yourself with something infinite. It is giving your entire being — body, vital, mind, heart and soul. What you have and what you are, you are giving to a divine cause.[178]

In limited self-giving we feel that we are superior and others are inferior. We may pity somebody, but while doing so we remain on the Himalayan heights and we see the person to whom we are showing pity at the bottom of a chasm. We stand millions of miles higher than the heartbreaking reality of the other person.

When charity is based on unconditional self-offering, on the other hand, we feel that the poor and the sick are like our little brothers and sisters. In a family, there can be no superiority and no inferiority. It is all oneness. The older brother will share what he has with his little brother, not because he pities him, but because he has compassion for him. When we show compassion, at that time our whole being becomes one with the suffering of others. If somebody is poverty-stricken and we offer our compassion, we become one with his poverty itself. We just come to him and become one with his problems.[179]

Question: What is real selfless service?

Sri Chinmoy: Real selfless service is that which does not expect a favourable result. Selfless service is only for the sake of self-giving; the result will come naturally. If there is an action, there will be a reaction. But the action will be performed not to please ourselves in our own way, but to please God in His own Way. We shall act when we are inspired from within. We shall work soulfully and consciously. If we work without inspiration, then we are working mechanically, like workers in a factory who do not want to be there. We have become another machine. Selfless service is not like that. It is cheerful, soulful, conscious and constant. First it is soulful service; then it is selfless; and finally, when it becomes unconditional and uncaring for the result, then it becomes perfect selfless service.[180]

Question: How do you know that you are really giving from the soul and not just fooling yourself?

Sri Chinmoy: If you give from the soul, you will not look to see whether or not the other person is receiving and you will not expect gratitude or appreciation from the other person. If you give something from the soul, you feel spontaneous joy just from the giving itself. You do not feel that you are giving something away; you are giving your smile or something else just because you feel an inner, spontaneous urge. When you are giving in an ordinary way, sometimes the idea of charity or a kind of superior feeling comes to your mind. You feel that you are superior because you are the one who is giving. But in real self-giving, you do not see the other person as somebody else, but rather as an extension of your own self. In giving yourself you are actually multiplying yourself. You are going from one to two. With your heart's oneness you are creating another self that is exactly like you, and to that other self you are giving the same things that you have. With your own divinity, you are creating another divinity exactly like yourself.[181]

Question: How are power and self-giving related?

Sri Chinmoy: The divine definition of power is self-giving: conscious, constant, cheerful, soulful, unconditional self-giving. Possessing is a form of power and self-giving is a form of power. Possessing is the human definition of power and self-giving is the divine definition of power.

What is self-giving? Self-giving is nothing other than God-becoming. If you give something divine, where does it come from? It comes from God Himself. So through self-giving we grow into the very image of God.[182]

Why Be Self-Giving?

The human life is nothing
But
A prison of misunderstandings.
How can we escape?
We can escape
Through the self-giving windows.[183]

I am a seeker. That means I pray and meditate, and I practise my peace-life. I consciously try to live a life of self-giving, for I know that this is the only way to get peace of mind. If I can walk soulfully, devotedly and unconditionally along the path of self-giving, then I will be a perfect stranger to frustration and self-contradiction. Right now my life is all self-contradiction. This moment my inner being is flooded with faith; the next moment teeming doubts are covering my entire mind. Always I hear the song of self-contradiction. But if I can offer my life to the Supreme in others consciously, devotedly and unconditionally, and become the very breath of self-giving, then I will have no frustration or self-contradiction.[184]

The more we give, the more we are appreciated. Think of a growing tree. A tree has flowers, fruits, leaves, branches and a trunk. But the tree gets real satisfaction not by possessing its capacity but by offering its capacity.

We, also, get real satisfaction by self-giving and not by keeping everything for our own use. The ego always tries to possess things for itself. But when we transcend ego we try to give everything for God's Satisfaction, for the world's satisfaction and for our soul's satisfaction. On the human level the ego tries to get satisfaction by using things for its own purpose. In the spiritual life, we transcend the human ego and then we use those things for a divine purpose, for the satisfaction of the entire world.[185]

We want happiness — happiness from life and happiness in life — and we want to offer this happiness to our near and dear ones. In order to achieve happiness in life, we have to give unreservedly what we have and what we are.

We feel that everything in life disappoints us and deserts us with the exception of one thing, and that thing is Truth. To live in Truth is to live in happiness. There are various ways to achieve this Truth in life. But only one way is most effective and that way is the way of self-giving — unreserved and unconditional self-giving to our own extended, expanded, enlarged, boundless, unlimited existence.

When we enter into our unlimited existence, we feel that we are of the One and for the many. At the same time we feel that we are in the many, for the One. This moment we are the tree; next moment we are the branches

We know that there also must be a root to the tree. We have to live in the root and this root is happiness. How can we live in the root all the time? We can live in the root only by self-giving: giving what we have and what we are. What we have is love and what we are is oneness. By offering love in any form to mankind — to our so-called superiors and so-called inferiors, or to our brothers and sisters of the world — we come to know what we ultimately and eternally are: oneness inseparable.[186]

How Can We Become Self-Giving?

To love others, to serve others, try to love and serve God first. Then automatically you will be in a position to love and serve all human beings, your brothers and sisters.[187]

The more we give to humanity, the sooner we grow into our larger than the largest heart. In an ordinary sense, when we spend five minutes with someone, we feel that we have given them eternity. Then again, if we like or love someone and we stay with them for five hours, we feel that we have given only five seconds. This is our way of thinking. If we love someone, two hours becomes one minute and if we do not like someone, one minute seems like two hours. So when we are in the physical or when we are in the mind, and we offer ourselves, we give an iota of our existence and immediately we feel that we have given the equivalent of one million dollars. But when we are in our heart, we will feel that we have so much more to give, so much more to give — our love, our peace, our light, our bliss. We will feel that what we have given is next to nothing.

So when it is a matter of self-giving, when we are in the mental world, we feel that it is a waste of time. We feel that we are just wasting our energy. But when we are in our heart, we feel that we have much more to give. We feel that our self-giving can never come to an end. We say, "Let the person come again. I will give him more, more, more."

When you remain in the heart, self-giving has divine reality in it; it is inexhaustible. The qualities that we are offering—joy, love, goodwill, concern—are absolutely infinite. Anything divine you have in infinite measure, provided your self-giving comes from the heart. If it comes from the mind, you will give practically nothing, but you will feel that you

95

have given everything. At that time, what is the use of self-giving?

When you give from the heart, you always feel, "I am a fool! I could have given much more, much more." Self-giving in the heart always unites us with vastness. Self-giving in the mind always binds us and blinds us. It makes us miserable. We regret it because we feel that we have wasted our precious time. But when we give from the heart, we feel an endless supply of joy, light and so many other divine qualities.

So when you perform an act of self-giving, always feel that it is coming from the heart and not from the mind.[188]

Each day we are granted by the Author of all good, out of His infinite Bounty, confidence both in our inner life and in our outer life. But if we use our physical mind — our earth-bound, sophisticated, obscure, unlit, unaspiring, intellectual mind — to search, we may not feel God's Confidence-Light. For the earth-bound mind feels that it is complete in itself; it does not need any reality other than its own existence.

But the heart constantly feels that it can house something more, that it can see something more, that it can grow into something more, that it has something more to offer to the world at large. The heart has the eagerness to receive and to achieve from the world within and from the world without. The heart has a constant, inner thirst to be universal, to be transcendental. Therefore, the heart always looks within and around to grasp and invoke the infinite Realities that abide in God's entire creation.

The heart comes to realise that there is only one way to achieve and grow into these infinite Realities and that is the way of self-giving. What is self-giving today, tomorrow that very thing is God-becoming. On the strength of self-giving, our aspiring heart becomes both universal and transcendental. This self-giving heart has a source of its own and that source is confidence. Confidence also has its source. Its source is God's Compassion, God's infinite, unconditional, immortal Compassion in man, for man.[189]

Question: How can we learn what is really important in life?

Sri Chinmoy: What is really important in life is self-giving. To whom do we give ourselves? We give ourselves to God inside all human beings. How do we do that? We do that by feeling that there is no other way to become happy and fulfilled in life.[190]

Question: How can I become self-giving with spontaneity and joy?

Sri Chinmoy: Joy, spontaneity and self-giving always go together. If one has a joyful heart, that means that one possesses spontaneity or a spontaneous heart and also that one is self-giving. Or we can say that self-giving is the hyphen, the connecting link, between joy and spontaneity. So, if one wants to be constantly self-giving to the omniscient, omnipresent, omnipotent Reality, then one has to constantly cultivate inner joy. Inside this inner joy, without fail one will find self-giving, and this self-giving embodies both spontaneity and joy.

How can you become self-giving? You can become self-giving by constantly feeling joy in every part of your existence from the sole of your foot to the crown of your head. If you can feel that a river is flowing in and through you carrying the message of joy, then automatically and spontaneously you can become self-giving in whatever you say, do or grow into.[191]

Question: How can I become more self-giving?

Sri Chinmoy: Whenever you do something, feel that you are giving of yourself. The other day I told you that when you give a glass of juice to a customer in your store, you have to repeat the name of the Supreme once, at least once. When you give that juice, feel that you are not just giving a liquid substance and a paper cup to some individual. No! You have to feel that you are giving to the Supreme Himself, to the One whom you are invoking and adoring. When you feel that you are giving it to the Supreme Himself, then naturally utmost devotion and surrender comes. At that time, your whole existence is entering into the Supreme in that person.

The best form of art is self-giving with the clear vision of whom you are giving to. You are not giving to the individual, but to the living embodiment of the Supreme or to the Supreme Himself whom you are seeing inside the person. If self-giving is done in that way, at every second every action of yours becomes the supreme art, and life itself becomes the supreme art.[192]

Self-Giving on the Outer Plane

First use your imagination-power
    To create a better world.
Then sleeplessly serve
    The present world
To turn your imagination
    Into reality.[193]

Question: What is a winning attitude?

Sri Chinmoy: A winning attitude, from the spiritual point of view, is a self-giving attitude. If you have a sincere self-giving attitude, then you are more than ready to conquer your own ignorance. In ordinary human life we try to win by defeating others. In the spiritual life we try to win by conquering the unaspiring and the undivine in ourselves. The winning attitude is our eagerness to conquer the qualities that are not willing to progress or that are trying to destroy us.[194]

Question: How should we think of self-giving on the outer plane?

Sri Chinmoy: Self-giving can take various forms on the outer plane. Here we are dealing with many individuals. If we find it difficult to give ourselves to many individuals, at least we can have an attitude of forgiveness. We forgive in order to make forward progress.

If we have so-called enemies, then we will all the time harbour evil thoughts towards our enemies. When we feel that we have enemies around us we actually forget our own goal. We think only of our enemies — how to conquer them, how to annihilate them. This becomes our goal. Then what kind of progress are we going to make?

So the best attitude is to always think of the ultimate Goal. This Goal is always found in self-giving. The more we can give soulfully, the sooner we shall get satisfaction in what we are doing or what we are growing into. Each individual knows how to offer some things to the world at large. Each individual knows how to offer something to his body, vital, mind, heart and soul. Only we have to do it.

We create thoughts, ideas and ideals. Let us say that a thought has entered into our mind. Immediately if we want to nourish that thought, we can put a good feeling into the thought. And that feeling comes from the heart itself. If we do not nourish the thought with our heart's psychic feelings, the thought remains powerless, it remains unfulfilled. Here we are talking about attitudes on the mental plane. But the real divinity, or the real essence of anything divine, lies only inside the heart. So anything that we see in the form of creation or anything that we create ourselves must be nourished by the feelings of the heart.

At every moment we can be attacked by negative thoughts, assailed by undivine thoughts. Again, at every moment with our inner will we can create good thoughts, loving thoughts, illumining thoughts, fulfilling thoughts. These thoughts can only function properly when we have an inner feeling from the heart.

The feelings of the heart we can increase only by self-giving. Right now we use the term 'self-giving' precisely because we have not sufficiently cultivated or developed the capacity that makes us feel that we are of the One and for the many. We have not yet discovered our universal oneness. But once we have discovered our oneness with the rest of the world, then it is not self-giving; it is only the fulfilment of our own inner awakening. When my hand does something for my leg or vice versa, they do not take it as self-giving. Hand and leg are part and parcel of one reality; they are one reality.

Unfortunately, at the present state of our evolution, our limited vision has not granted us the capacity to feel everyone as our own. So let us start with the idea of self-giving. We shall give what we have and what we are; we shall give our good thoughts.[195]

Inner Progress

My life is only half full
When I receive.
My heart is completely full
Only when I give.[196]

A man of desire wants to dominate the world. He wants the whole world to surrender to him. A man of aspiration wants to establish his universal oneness-heart with the rest of the world. How? On the strength of his self-giving, which is the only way to bring about world peace.[197]

We start our journey with the desire-life. The desire-life helps to free us from the world of sloth, inertia and ignorance. Then we come to the aspiration-life. The aspiration-life helps us to reach higher goals, higher ideals and higher realisations. The self-giving life constantly makes us feel that we are of the One and for the One. Him to please in His own Way is our sole choice.[198]

The human in us constantly cries for success, more success, abundant success. But the divine in us wants progress, constant progress, inner and outer. This progress is founded entirely upon self-giving, and self-giving is the precursor of God-becoming.

The human in us wants to possess the world so it can utilise the world in its own way. Alas, to its extreme sorrow it sees that before it possesses the world, the world has already possessed it mercilessly. The divine in us wants to offer its very existence to the world; it wants to illumine the world with its love and selfless dedication. Lo and behold, it sees that before it has illumined the world, the world has illumined it totally.[199]

Progress, which is founded upon self-giving, is something continuous. This progress does not offer pride to the seeker in us. It only makes us feel that we are moving on our spiritual journey, walking along Eternity's Road. Each time progress touches the goal, it sees a new goal farther beyond. It is constantly transcending its own reality-existence. Eventually, when this ever-transcending process reaches God, it finds that God also is progressing, ever transcending His own Reality-Existence.[200]

In ugliness there is beauty, in imperfection there is beauty, in everything that exists in God's universe there is beauty. Again, beauty has its degrees, and when we become conscious seekers, we aim at the highest beauty, at the perfect Perfection of beauty. This beauty looms large in us only when we become conscious and constant divine soldiers of self-giving. When possessiveness leaves us and selflessness takes its place, the beauty of the transcendental Height enters into our life of aspiration. Today what we call self-giving, tomorrow that very thing we call God-becoming, which is beauty unparalleled. Self-giving is the flowering of our love divine. God-becoming is the ultimate blossoming of our dedicated, devoted and unconditional surrender to the Inner Pilot.[201]

Question: How can we cultivate the inner silence so that we can know God's Will?

Sri Chinmoy: I fully approve of your cultivating the inner silence. But why do you have to adopt such a difficult method when there is an easier process? The easier process is self-giving. Just give yourself totally and then see whether you are carried away by the waves or whether you become the ocean itself. That is the easiest and most effective way. One way is to dig, dig, dig and God knows when you are going to glimpse a tiny drop of water. The other way is just to throw yourself, let us say, into the sea of peace, and not worry whether you will meet water animals or jewels inside. The one way takes time and is very uncertain. While you are digging, if you do not get a glimpse of water or consciousness, let us say, then you will be disappointed. But the other way, if you go slowly and steadily by giving yourself, throwing yourself into the sea of self-dedication, then you are getting real satisfaction out of life.[202]

Question: How can we feel that our soul is accompanying us in all our activities?

Sri Chinmoy: If you are doing all your activities prayerfully, soulfully and self-givingly, then you are bound to feel that your soul is accompanying you.[203]

Self-Giving as Spiritual Practice

Every day
I may not feel like
*   Serving others.*
Still, I do serve,
Just for the purification
*   Of my body*
And for the satisfaction
*   Of my soul.*[204]

A seeker knows and feels that he can live without food, without water, without air, without everything on earth, but he cannot live without God's Compassion. God's Compassion is the seeker's Immortality. When he starts drinking the nectar of this Immortality, then he realises himself. When he realises himself, he feels that in and through him God is manifesting His highest Reality, that God is singing His Song of Eternity and dancing His Dance of Immortality. When a seeker drinks ambrosia, he feels that Heaven is not somewhere else. Heaven is in his consciousness. We do not have to go to a particular state or country or kingdom called Heaven. No! Heaven, which is perpetual life, the infinite life within us, is a state of consciousness. This consciousness an aspiring seeker is bound to attain when he drinks nectar. And this nectar he gets on the strength of his self-giving, his unconditional self-giving.[205]

I was a student of prayer, but I cannot say that I enjoyed my studies. When I was a student of prayer, anxiety and worry killed me. At times even fear and doubt killed me. Then I became a student of meditation. When I was a student of meditation, at times I had confidence in my meditation, and at times I totally lacked confidence. Therefore, I did not succeed in a striking manner. Because meditation is all peace-expansion, light-expansion, love-expansion and oneness-expansion, I could have progressed fast, very fast. But I did not.

When I became a student of self-giving, I discovered immediately that my self-giving was growing into something infinitely more than I had ever dreamed of, something that I never would have had the capacity to acquire. What was it? A fruitful life of God-becoming vision-light and God-manifesting manifestation-delight.

I want to remain only a student of self-giving. The other two I do not want, I do not need separately. I do not need them as a separate existence in my self-giving. My self-giving includes meditation, prayer, everything. Therefore, what I need always is a self-giving cry and a self-giving smile.[206]

My Beloved Lord, my Beloved Friend, my Beloved All, You have given me my simplicity, You have given me my sincerity, You Have given me my serenity, You have given my purity.

Simplicity You have given me so that I can start the pilgrimage along the road of my body-consciousness. Sincerity You have given me so that I can start my pilgrimage along the road of my vital-dynamism. Serenity You have given me so that I can start my pilgrimage along the road of my mental vision. Purity You have given me so that I can start my pilgrimage along the road of my heart's delight.

My Lord Supreme, You have also told me that my simplicity, sincerity, serenity and purity will reach their acme of perfection only when my heart's gratitude flowers petal by petal, blossoming into perfect Perfection. And for that what I need is constant self-giving — conscious, soulful and unconditional self-giving. In order to have conscious, constant and unconditional self-giving, what I need is a real approach to You — not as a beggar but as a lover; not as a beggar-destitute but as a lover-friend. If I approach You as a beggar, You will give me what I need or what I want. But my receptivity-vessel is so small that even if You give me what I need, it will not be much, it will be far from my full satisfaction. And if You give me what I want, it may not be the right thing. You will give me, but what You give me will ultimately be a source of frustration and never a source of satisfaction.

My Lord Supreme, even if You give me an iota of what You want to give me, that very iota will not only please the real in me, the soul, but immortalise the human in me. The human in me is my human hope, my earthly hope. Hope before it bears fruit is nothing short of illusion and delusion — mental hallucination, to say the least. But even this very hope You will be able to immortalise. Once my hope is immortalised, I shall see my hope in the form of Your own Reality's Vision, transcendental Vision, and Your own Vision's Reality, universal Reality.[207]

In the spiritual life, the higher we go, the greater is our self-offering. This self-offering is not an act of self-aggrandisement. We offer ourselves because we feel that only by offering what we have and what we are can we become totally one with the rest of the world. There is no feeling of superiority; there is only a feeling of oneness. And this feeling of oneness comes from the soul. When the soul's light is offered to the world at large, it takes the form of humility. The seekers of the infinite Truth have to bend down to offer something to unaspiring, sleeping humanity. This humility of ours comes only from sincere aspiration. In sincere aspiration we see light and grow into light. And this light has to be spread. It can be spread only when we have a genuine concern for the manifestation of God on earth. So when we have peace, light and bliss, we have to offer them. The act of self-offering is a manifestation of God; and self-offering is achieved through humility, which is the light of the soul.[208]

Question: How would you define spiritual goals?

Sri Chinmoy: According to my inner conviction, spirituality is at once self-giving and God-becoming. This self-giving is not an offering to somebody else, to a third party; it is an offering to one's own higher self. Self-giving is nothing short of an act of self-uncovering, which is another name for self-discovering. And self-discovering blossoms into God-becoming.

What is God-becoming? Each individual will have an answer of his own in accordance with his soul's development and his life's needs. My inner conviction is that God-becoming is the soulful recovery of one's own forgotten self. God-becoming is the fruitful discovery and soulful acceptance of this realisation: "In my yesterday's life, I had; in my today's life, I am. What did I have? God the man as the aspiring seed. What have I become? Man the God as the fulfilling fruit."[209]

Service from a Lofty Viewpoint

A true seeker is he who loves, serves, becomes and eternally is. He is a seeker who wants to realise the highest transcendental Truth, who wants to claim God as his very own, who wants to offer all that he has and all that he is. What he has, is love for God; who he is, is concern for humanity. The seeker's role is of paramount importance both in Heaven and on earth.

Service, from the spiritual point of view, is self-giving. Now, this self-giving has to be sincere, direct, spontaneous, unreserved and unconditional. When our service is sincere, the world-body needs and utilises our service. When our service is direct, the world-vital needs and utilises our service. When our service is spontaneous, the world-mind needs and utilises our service. When our service is unreserved, the world-heart needs and utilises our service. Finally, when our service is unconditional, the world-soul needs and utilises our service.

Service is self-expansion. A sincere seeker serves precisely because he knows that there is and there can be nothing other than service. When he serves aspiring humanity, it is because his inner necessity commands him to serve. Each seeker has to be true to himself all the time. It is easy for him to fool the world around him, but if he is not sincere to himself, God-realisation will always remain a far cry.

Before we become sincere seekers, we follow the path of ego. Ego is our self-made human reality. This reality has to be transformed, or illumined and perfected. Otherwise, before we know it, the ego will destroy our ideals and our inner potentiality

Service is self-purification. Self-purification is the precursor of the physical nature's transformation. The transformation of the physical nature and God-manifestation are inseparable, like the obverse and the reverse of the same coin. The transformation of the physical and the manifestation of the spiritual always go side by side. Transformation is the dream-fulfilled reality on earth; manifestation is the reality-fulfilled Dream in Heaven.

Service is God-receiving. We receive God with the devotion of our body, with the purity of our vital, with the eagerness of our mind, with the oneness of our heart and with the vastness of our soul.[210]

Chapter 6

FORGIVENESS

Forgiveness for Ourselves and Others

Forgiveness means transformation
Of a human heart into a divine life.[211]

Forgiveness is a powerful divine force. To forgive others in the physical plane is a difficult task. To forget others' imperfections is more difficult. Not to notice anything wrong in others is most difficult. But when we think of God it becomes easy for us to forgive others; when we pray to God it becomes easy to forget others' shortcomings, limitations and imperfections. When we meditate on God, it becomes easy for us not to notice anything wrong in others.[212]

When we do something wrong God's Forgiveness does its duty. That is to say, God forgives us. But our forgiveness does not play its role. We torment our very existence. This does not mean that God wants to escape from reality just by forgiving us. And it does not mean that we are just, therefore we are not forgiving ourselves. God feels that each time He forgives us, He gives us another opportunity to walk along Divinity's road and reach our destined Goal.

But when we do not forgive ourselves, the ignorance in us which caused the mistake gets another opportunity to delay our progress. It prevents us from starting our journey fresh. When we make a mistake, if we torment ourselves in the name of justice, in this way we delay and delay; we do not start our journey over again..

When we do something wrong, immediately we have to

forgive ourselves as God forgives us. We must decide not to commit the mistake again, and at the same time we must embrace the new opportunity to do absolutely the right thing. Just because I have entered into a dark room, if I go on saying and thinking, "I was in a dark room! I was in a dark room!" then I will not be able to come out of the consciousness of that dark room and enter into the room that is illumined. Since God gives us the opportunity to leave the dark room and enter the room of illumination, we must accept that opportunity and utilise it properly.[213]

If we want to make ourselves truly happy, perfectly happy, unimaginably happy, then we must develop the power of forgiveness. And this forgiveness not only shall we apply to people who have done wrong things to us, but also we shall have to apply most powerfully to ourselves. We have to forgive ourselves for all the bad things we have done. Otherwise, we will not be able to go forward — never, never!

If we do not forgive ourselves for what we did ten years ago, then what will happen? Our guilty conscience will be like ten dead elephants that we have to drag along with us. If we want to have deer speed, then we shall not only forgive others, but we shall also forgive ourselves. In order to be truly happy, unimaginably happy, infinitely happy, we have to apply forgiveness both to the world around us and to ourselves.

Forgiveness is of utmost importance. Forgive the world around you, those who have done something wrong to you, and forgive yourself for what you have done, but with the view that you will not commit the same mistake again.

Before, you committed the mistake of not identifying your-self with the whole world. That is why forgiving the world was such a difficult task. But forgiveness becomes easier than the easiest if we take the right attitude, which is that we have to go forward, we have to go forward, we have to go forward. We cannot allow the weight of dead elephants to make us fall behind all the time.

The quickest method to become happy is to forgive the world. Sooner than the soonest the miracle-power of forgiveness will give us happiness.[214]

Question: How can we remember to forgive the world for its defects and to forgive ourselves for our own defects?

Sri Chinmoy: If others do something wrong, if we do not forgive them, if we harbour undivine thoughts against them or want to punish them, we will never find true satisfaction. In order to satisfy ourselves, our reality, we must forgive others. Forgiveness is illumination. We have to feel that by forgiving others we are illumining ourselves, our own enlarged, expanded Self.

If we do not forgive, what happens? We place a heavy load on our shoulders. If I have done something wrong and I do not try to forgive myself or illumine myself, I will harbour the idea that I have made a mistake. Each time I think of my wrong action I will add to my heavy load of guilt. Similarly, if others have done me an act of injustice, the more I think of this the heavier becomes my load of anger and resentment.

It is always advisable to forgive others and to forgive oneself. Again, we have to know who is forgiving whom? I as an individual have no right to forgive others or even to forgive myself. It is the Divine within me that is inspiring me to raise my consciousness to light, to higher light, to highest Light. An act of forgiveness means a movement to a higher reality. And when we reach the highest Reality, we become one with the omnipresent Reality.

We are all integral parts of a living organism. If I have only two arms, I am incomplete; I need two legs, too. I need everything in order to be complete, perfect and whole. So I have to accept others as my very own. First I accept them and then I transform them. And whom am I transforming if not my own expanding, enlarged reality?[215]

Question: How do you forgive injustice?

Sri Chinmoy: When we think of injustice in human terms, we have to go to the very depths of our realisation. When we came into the world we made a solemn promise to God that we would realise God, manifest God and fulfil God here on earth. This was our most sincere, most soulful promise to God. When we made that promise we were in the soul's world. We did not have the physical body; our real existence was the soul. At that time the soul said, "I am descending into the world only to please You, to fulfil You, to manifest You unconditionally." But now, the word 'unconditionally' immediately frightens us. It is a poisonous word; we cannot use it. All is conditional, conditional.

These people whom you feel are very unjust have done something undivine, true. But look at your own promise. You expect from these people perfection; you feel they have to do everything in a perfect way. But perfection comes only when we fulfil our promise. Our first and foremost promise was to God, to please Him and fulfil Him on earth. We have not fulfilled our promise; yet we expect others to fulfil their promise. As spiritual people, we should always see what we have done wrong. Millions of things we have done wrong. If we do millions of things wrong, then naturally God is forgiving us. Otherwise, we would not be able to exist on earth. If He is ready to forgive us in spite of our countless defects and mistakes, how is it that we cannot forgive someone else?

A spiritual seeker immediately claims himself to be a chosen child of God. An unaspiring person, a person who is wallowing in the pleasures of ignorance, would never dare to claim this. He does not dare to claim God as his very own. But you do dare to claim that you are God's chosen child, just because you have got an iota of God's good qualities. God is good, God is divine, God is perfect, and all His divine qualities you have to some extent. So if one of God's qualities is forgiveness, and if God forgives you twenty-four hours a day, can you not forgive a person for one second? If your Source has the capacity to do something in infinite measure, naturally you also should have the capacity to forgive or illumine others who have done something wrong, according to your standard.[216]

Question: If you want to offer your best wishes to a friend who lives far away, and then through negligence you miss their birthday, is it too late afterwards, or can you make up for it?

Sri Chinmoy: Better late than never. Your friends will forgive you, because they know that these things happen. It is not something uncommon. But if you have a very strong inner connection with that person, it will be difficult for you to forgive yourself.

Many times it happens that we can forgive others, but we cannot forgive ourselves because we expect something infinitely more beautiful, more soulful, more powerful from ourselves. Ordinary, unaspiring people forgive themselves. Then as soon as they see the same fault in somebody else, they can never forgive that person. But when good people see an iota of imperfection in themselves, they get so mad at themselves. When bad people see a little imperfection in others, they try to make it larger than the largest. That is the difference between a good person and a bad person. A good person will try to forgive or ignore the other person's faults. He will say, "Poor fellow! I also have imperfections." A bad person always tries to hide his own imperfections. He tries to only look at the imperfections of others. A good person looks at his own little imperfection and says, "If I have this imperfection, how am I going to become God's dearest, most perfect instrument?" He does not want to forgive himself. He wants to perfect himself at every moment.

If you do not offer your good wishes to your friends, if you are a good person, you will suffer infinitely more than the person who has not received the card from you. For this reason you have to be always very careful. If you have already made the mistake, then call the person or write to the person and apologise profusely. If there is sincerity in your heart, it will definitely touch their heart.

Your inner sincerity is the most important thing. First of all, if your connection with that person is very deep, you will not forget. But if you have forgotten, then apologise. If it comes from the very depths of your heart, from your inner being, the other person will feel that it was a deplorable mistake and in no way did you want to ignore them.[217]

Question: What is the connection between compassion and forgiveness?

Sri Chinmoy: Compassion and forgiveness are two different things. Let us say a mischievous little boy strikes you unnecessarily hard. You can strike him much harder, but you do not. Why? Because you have forgiven him. Then you see another little boy, all alone. He is unable to cross the street by himself because he is afraid. At that time you go and help him. You wait for the light and you take him across the street. This is your compassion. So this is how you can separate compassion from forgiveness. Somebody needs your help, and you have the strength, you have the capacity, to be of service to him. At that time you are showing your compassion. Somebody else is unable to conquer their wrong forces. There you are offering your forgiveness. These two divine qualities are of supreme necessity every day in our life. The Supreme has Compassion and Forgiveness in infinite measure. With His Compassion-Eye He follows us everywhere. Again with His Forgiveness-Heart, He forgives all our wrong thoughts and actions.[218]

Forgiving Our Parents and Children Especially

To become a happiness-fountain,
I must forgive those
Who ruthlessly hurt me
Every day.[219]

Question: What if your childhood experiences were of suffering rather than sweetness?

Sri Chinmoy: If you feel that your parents were not nice, if you did not get good treatment from your parents right from your infancy, then you have to take your imagination as a reality. Imagine once again your childhood. You were brought up in one family, but right around you, in your vicinity, some parents were extremely, extremely nice to their children. Identify with them, identify, identify! This is not a false approach. Your parents brought you into the world, true, but I wish to say that imagination is a reality of its own.

Always try identification. You did not receive love and affection, perhaps, but now you can definitely apply your imagination and imagine love and affection. Just think of one particular family where the parents were so indulgent to their children. That imagination will definitely give you sweetness, happiness and a feeling of inner fulfilment. Just spread your imagination-wings! You are like a bird. Spread your wings and just fly to a country, imagine a village and see a particular place. What you are seeing is so true!

If your parents were not kind, just imagine sweetness, sweetness, sweetness. Early in the morning, look at a flower, look at the dawn. If you can identify yourself with nature, you are getting tremendous joy. At that time, are you thinking about how your parents struck you black and blue? You are the same person, but your wisdom has to work. You have to bring forward sweet memories, sweet memories, sweet memories. If you do not have sweet memories in your immediate family, that cannot prevent you from getting sweetness from your childhood.

Now that you are mature, you have to use wisdom at every moment. Sometimes in a family, parents get angry. They stop their children when they want to go to university, or they do not pay the costs. In the end, if one accepts the spiritual life, it means one has to forgive them. It is very difficult sometimes, when we do not forgive a person, to bring sweetness out of our memories of that person.

If your parents were not nice, first forgive them. By harbouring bitter memories of your parents' so-called misconduct, you will never be able to bring your own inner sweetness to the fore. You have to forgive your parents and forget the sad experience. If absolute necessity demands, you may even have to forget about your parents. Only try to imagine yourself, with your consciousness as a seven-year-old, to see how children elsewhere were given tremendous affection, sweetness and fondness.[220]

Question: I find it difficult to have emotional contact with my daughter.

Sri Chinmoy: Please think of yourself when you were her age. Try to see if you were also unruly or whether you had the same difficulties and shortcomings that you find difficult to put up with in your daughter. When you were her age, if you also had them, then feel yourself as a larger part of her existence. Once you did something and now your daughter is doing it. When you did it, your parents had to put up with it, and now you have to put up with it in your daughter.

If you were not like that when you were her age, then look around at your friends and neighbours. You will see that their children are infinitely worse than your daughter. Then you will thank God. So if you were the same when you were her age, then let your compassion come to the fore. If you were not of her type, just compare her with other children of her age. Look around and you will see many, many children who are very undivine, very hostile. Then you will have the consolation that at least you do not have to start from their level, then you will have some joy, and this will be your strength. With this strength you will be able to forgive your daughter and with new courage and inspiration you will be able to work with her.[221]

Friendship and Forgiveness

He who has
The abundant capacity
To forgive others
Sees that he has
Nobody to forgive.[222]

Question: Recently you said we should strengthen our friendships.

Sri Chinmoy: True friendship is very rare, but it does exist. I cherish those people who are true friends. I am not asking you to have the whole world as your friend — far from it. Only two or three real friends are needed. Even if you have only one friend, it helps considerably.

Friendship is based on forgiveness. Today if your friend has done something wrong, you have to forgive her immediately by thinking that you could have made the same mistake. If she has been nasty to you today, you have to forgive her immediately. Tomorrow you may be in the same position — you could be nasty to her. So if you forgive her when she is nasty, then if a day comes when you are equally nasty, she will forgive you. Good qualities eventually come forward. Good qualities will not remain dormant forever and forever. Unfortunately, good qualities take more time to come to the fore than bad qualities. The divine forces will eventually be victorious, but in the meantime, the undivine forces make us feel that they have conquered us.

I always feel the supreme need for friendship. The Absolute Supreme is our only Friend, but He tells us on the earthly level, for earthly purposes, we need one or two individuals with whom we can share our sufferings and our joys. As soon as we share our suffering, it is gone. As soon as we share our joy, it doubles. Our sadness is a heavy load. If someone comes to share it with us, it reduces the burden. If you are carrying twenty pounds on your shoulder and if your friend comes and takes ten pounds from you, then together you can walk along easily. But if you do not tell the person about your suffering, then you are carrying the whole twenty pounds by yourself.[223]

Question: How can we become more tolerant of our friends' wrong actions?

Sri Chinmoy: First think of how many millions of things you have done wrong since you have been in this body. You will be able to count at least ten undivine things. Out of millions of things you have probably done wrong, you will be sincere enough to admit at least ten things. Then ask yourself if anybody has forgiven you. Naturally God has forgiven you. If

He had not forgiven you, by this time you would have been in the other world. But when somebody else does something wrong, you become angry and want to punish that person. Try to count how many things that person has done wrong to you. He may have done many, many things wrong in his life but perhaps he has done only two things wrong to you; whereas you are the culprit for at least ten individual items, and the Supreme has forgiven you.

God exercises forgiveness. In your case and my case, what we exercise will be called the strength of oneness. Yesterday I did something wrong, and God forgave me. How is it that today I cannot identify myself with someone else and feel that the very thing that he has done, I could have done? What he has done wrong today, I can easily do tomorrow. I should be grateful to God that I did not do it today, and remember that tomorrow there is every possibility that I will do that very same thing.

We should sympathise with the person who has done something wrong, or, on the strength of our oneness, we should tolerate it. Toleration is not an act of weakness. Far from it! Toleration is the acceptance of reality at a different level of consciousness. Mother Earth, the trees, the oceans and the mountains, do they not tolerate us? We do many, many things wrong; we abuse them in millions of ways. Yet they forgive us and nourish us continually.[224]

Question: Will God help me if I ask Him to help me forgive a friend?

Sri Chinmoy: Now look, this child of yours in the bedroom cries for food. You are in the kitchen, but you run when you hear the cry of your child. The child may be anywhere, but why do you come running from the kitchen? Because you have heard his cry. We are God's children and when He hears our cry, He comes to us. He comes to help us. He cherishes us because we are helpless and because we need Him. When we have a true need and when we cry most sincerely, God will certainly come. He will give you compassion, strength and the power to forgive and love the person who hurt you. God will change that person because when you yourself change, the other person is changed, also.[225]

Question: Please tell me what to do when I feel rejection from my spiritual brothers and sisters.

Sri Chinmoy: When you feel rejected by your spiritual brothers and sisters, the human in you will be sad, frustrated and furious. But the divine within you will immediately pray to the Supreme for forgiveness for your brothers and sisters. The only way they will get illumination is if the Supreme forgives them.

Suppose I am your spiritual brother and I have rejected you. The human in you will immediately become furious and try to take revenge, or it may withdraw. You will want to have nothing to do with me because I have rejected you or insulted you. But at that time the divine in you will try to come forward with compassion because it knows that I have made a serious mistake in rejecting you. If you also reject me, tit for tat, then in what way are you superior to me? What I have done is wrong. It is very bad, true, but if you do not want to do the same wrong thing, then you have to forgive me and you have to ask God to forgive me as well.

The Saviour Christ prayed, "Father, forgive them, for they know not what they do." Similarly, you should pray to God on behalf of your brother or sister, who is the real culprit at that time. This is the first thing required. Secondly, you should pray to God for his illumination, so that he does not reject you or anyone else in the future. If he is really forgiven and illumined by the Supreme, then he will not reject you again.

But if you also play the same role, and reject someone who has rejected you, then both of you are going to be swimming in the sea of ignorance. He has done something wrong, and you are doing the same thing. Paying him back in his own coin does not serve any purpose. What you want, after all, is the illumination of your spiritual brothers and sisters.[226]

God's Forgiveness

Oh, my life's Love Supreme
Sleeplessly I invoke You
To forgive me today.
O great One, O world's Reality-Salvation,
May I be fully awakened
In purity's auspicious dawn.[227]

When you make a serious mistake, conscious or unconscious, immediately you have to cry for forgiveness. If you do not ask the Supreme for forgiveness, then the hostile or negative forces will increase and increase the power of your crime until it becomes an inner cancer and destroys your whole system. Then your own wrong forces will intensify and become worse and take the form of arrogance, false pride, callousness and carelessness.

So, with your aspiration, your prayer-life, your meditation-life, your dedication-life and your oneness-life with God's Will, you have to ask God to forgive you for all your mistakes, conscious and unconscious. You also have to ask Him to illumine your unconscious mistakes so that you will become aware of them and not make them again. Then God will illumine you so that your unconscious mistakes will come forward and you will say, "This was the thing that I did not take as a mistake or a weakness in my life." Through this kind of illumination you will be able to understand your unconscious mistakes and avoid repeating them.

Unfortunately, many people do not believe in God's Forgiveness. But if mistakes are not forgiven, then purification cannot take place in the body, vital, mind and heart. And if purity is not there, then there can be no receptivity in those parts of the being, and the divine forces that you are praying for will never be able to enter permanently into your life. Only if God forgives your mistakes and you do get purity in your entire consciousness will you be able to increase your receptivity and receive God's divine qualities in abundant measure.

So the best thing is: every day, before you go to sleep, to pray to the Supreme to forgive you for the things that you have done wrong. This is not the philosophy that says we are all sinners. No, only I am speaking of the conscious or unconscious mistakes that you make in your daily life. Pray to the Supreme for forgiveness and for the illumination of your unconscious mistakes.[228]

God, out of His infinite Bounty, forgives us immediately precisely because He feels that if He gives us another opportunity, we will be able to run, we will be able to fly and dive within. He does not forgive us out of negligence or carelessness or in order to avoid the issue. Far from it! He feels that each time we commit some Himalayan blunder, if He does not forgive us, then our progress comes to an end. Each forgiveness is an opportunity He grants us when we make a mistake. But in the name of justice, morality and so forth, we torture ourselves so that we cannot move ahead. God forgives us, but we just stick to our wrong action in the name of perfection in nature. Finally, it is we who are the losers.[229]

Question: When I feel unworthy, I doubt that God will forgive me. I do not see how I can expect to be forgiven in one short incarnation.

Sri Chinmoy: Ask yourself, is there any way we can defeat God? The answer is no. If God uses His Forgiveness-Power, then this Forgiveness-Power is infinitely stronger than all the misdeeds that you think you have done in this incarnation or even in your previous incarnations.

Think of a room that remains unlit for days or even months. Then you come in and turn on the switch, and in the twinkling of an eye you get back the light. Similarly, you have to feel that your weakness is nothing, nothing, in comparison to God's Compassion-Power or Forgiveness-Power.

Now the question is, you say, why should God forgive you if you repeatedly do the same wrong thing? Today you do the wrong thing and then you pray to God, "O Lord, forgive me, forgive me, forgive me!" Then again tomorrow you may do the same thing. It is like a person who eats chili. Today he says, "My tongue is burning! I will not take chili anymore." Then again the next day he takes chili and again he burns his tongue.

God will forgive us no matter how many times we do the wrong thing, if we have a sincere cry. But will He not be more pleased with us if we do not repeat the same wrong thing again and again? God's Forgiveness is always there, true, but God will be proud of us when we can give up the wrong things altogether.

If it is not possible to give them up overnight, then every day try to decrease the number of things that are wrong in your mind or in your outer life. You know how many times you are doing something wrong in your outer life or inner life. Count them. Then next day see if you are able to decrease the number. So like that, little by little, if you can decrease the number, a day will come when you will not make any mistake. At that time, God will not only be pleased; He will be very, very, very proud of you. Always remember that God's Compassion-Power is infinitely stronger than all the blunders you think you have made.[230]

Question: How do you receive God's Forgiveness?

Sri Chinmoy: You receive God's Forgiveness only by reminding yourself —constantly, consciously, sleeplessly and breathlessly — that God is Forgiveness Itself. You should not think of God as Justice or as infinite Light or Peace. You should not think of any other aspect of God. You should only think of God's Forgiveness or of God the Forgiveness. You have to inundate your mind and your heart with one thought: forgiveness, forgiveness, forgiveness. Instead of thinking of God's Justice-Light, you should just repeat, "My Lord is all Forgiveness, my Lord is all Forgiveness."

While repeating, "My Lord is all Forgiveness," you must not think of all the countless undivine things that you have done: "Oh, I have told a lie, I have struck someone, I have done so many other things wrong." No, you will see only the positive side. You will think only of God's Forgiveness before you, around you and within you. If hundreds and thousands of times you can repeat most soulfully, "My Lord is all Forgiveness, my Lord is all Forgiveness," then all your Himalayan blunders will be washed away. All the mistakes that you have made over the years, all the ignorant things that you have done, will be annihilated. At that time, you will not only feel that you are forgiven, but you will feel that you yourself are God's Forgiveness. If someone asks you your name, you will say, "My name is my Lord's Forgiveness." If someone asks who you are, you will say, "I am my Lord's Forgiveness."

This will be your only credential. In the ordinary life

people have many credentials. They have this university degree, that degree and so on. But a spiritual seeker will say that he has only one credential. He will say either, "I am my Lord's Forgiveness," or "I am my Lord's Compassion," or "I am my Lord's Love." So, if somebody asks what your credentials are, immediately you will say, "My Lord's Compassion is my only credential," or "My Lord's Forgiveness is my only credential." This is not just false humility, for in the inmost recesses of your heart you do feel that your only credential is God's Compassion or God's Forgiveness. That is what all seekers must feel.[231]

Question: How can I feel God's Protection all the time?

Sri Chinmoy: You have to pray for God's Protection. You cannot pray for twenty-four hours, but daily four or five times you can consciously pray for God's Protection.

And while you are praying for protection, you have to simultaneously pray for forgiveness. Protection comes quickly if you pray for forgiveness. Suppose you have done something wrong, either today, yesterday or ten years ago. If you want protection from God, God will say, "You want protection, but you have done a few things wrong. Have you asked Me for forgiveness?"

The best approach is to pray to God, "Please forgive me for the things that I have done wrong, and even for the things that I am going to do wrong tomorrow." You have no control over the future. God may protect you today, but the next moment you may be tempted to do something wrong. If you ask for forgiveness first and then ask for protection, protection will come faster, plus it will be more effective.[232]

Forgive and Forget

Forgive,
You will have happiness.
Forget,
You will have satisfaction.
Forgive and forget,
You will have everlasting peace
Within and without.[233]

Question: When something painful happens in my life, it affects my heart or, let us say, it breaks my heart. Then it is very, very hard for me to forget about it. I can actually forgive certain things pretty easily, but to forget about it is almost impossible for me.

Sri Chinmoy: Yes, it is true that to forgive someone is easier than to forget the experience. But we can take it as a challenge. To forgive is the first challenge. Suppose someone has done something very bad. I have taken up the challenge to forgive him, and I have succeeded. Then I have to accept another challenge — that I will forget what he has done.

It is like hurdles. The first challenge, let us say, is like a hill or a mountain which is not as high as the Himalayas. You have climbed up that mountain by forgiving the person. Then you are finding it difficult to forget the painful experience. You have to take it as another mountain which is higher. Even though it is higher, you cannot say that mountain is not climbable. You are saying that when somebody does an injustice to you, you forgive them. Many, many people cannot forgive. You should be proud of yourself that you have forgiven the person. The next challenge is to forget the incident. You have to take it as another mountain much higher than the previous one.

The key is love. You do not have to love the person. You have to love God infinitely more. Suppose somebody is your friend. He has done something bad, and you have forgiven him. You feel that is enough. Why should you go one step further and forget the experience? But the memory of that particular experience is killing you. From time to time it comes into your mind, and you think, "How can he be so bad? I have been so nice to him." At that time you have to forget about the person and only think of the Supreme. You have to ask yourself inwardly, "Does the Supreme want me to hold onto this experience, or does He want me to forget about the experience the way I have forgiven the person?" Then your Inner Pilot, the Supreme, will say, "This experience is causing suffering for you. From time to time it comes into your mind, and it destroys all your joy. Therefore I want you to forget it completely."

Then the best thing is to follow the Supreme's Way. He has inwardly inspired you to forgive the person, and you have forgiven him. If He says you must forget the experience, then you have to do it. Just because you love God and God always tells us, "Forgive, forgive, forgive," you have done the first part. The second part is to say, "Since I am suffering whenever I think of that experience, the best thing is to forget." You have to prove your love of God by forgetting. The more you can love God, the easier it becomes to forget the experience. In your case, your love of God has already come forward to a certain extent because you are ready to forgive the person. If you increase your own love for God, God will give you the capacity to forget the experience. It entirely depends on love.

Another way to tackle this question is by having sympathetic oneness, by saying, "If I had been in his place, perhaps I would have behaved worse. Poor fellow, on that day perhaps somebody insulted him or scolded him. Perhaps he was fired or something else of that nature took place." When people misbehave towards us, we have no idea what went through their mind or what happened in their life on that particular day. We judge a person by seeing his normal activities. For years and years we have observed someone. We have formed an opinion that he is a good person. All of a sudden why is he behaving so badly? Perhaps on that day something happened to destroy all his peace and joy. Perhaps he had become a victim to miseries, so he was emptying his miseries onto you. By nature that person is good, but on that day perhaps he became subject to some worries, anxieties or criticism. If we have sympathetic oneness, then we will know something has gone wrong in his life. Otherwise, he would not have misbehaved so badly. Then if we have more sympathetic oneness, we will say, "Perhaps I would have done worse. I also could have said unkind things to somebody who desperately needed to hear something nice from me."

When we establish sympathetic oneness, we see very few mistakes in the world. Always we see faults, because we feel that we are perfect while others are imperfect. But if we establish our oneness with others, we may see that we have more weaknesses than they have, because we have one extra weakness: we criticise them, while at the same time we are telling the world that we have established sympathy.[234]

Question: How does the Supreme illumine the past?

Sri Chinmoy: The Supreme illumines the past by forgiveness. Real forgiveness means forgetfulness, conscious forgetfulness. If somebody really forgives you for something that you did, then he will not keep the memory even in his inner vision. But if he does not forgive you, he keeps it in front of his inner vision. Illumination is necessary because of darkness. Mistakes are darkness. So, the Supreme illumines our mistakes through forgiveness.[235]

Is Forgiveness Ever a Mistake?

Sometimes you have to fight,
If God does not want you
To be humiliated by your enemy.

Sometimes you have to forgive,
If God wants you
To illumine your enemy.[236]

Question: Could you tell me if there is ever a right time for me to defend myself?

Sri Chinmoy: Before you defend yourself, you have to know whether you ought to defend yourself! If you do something wrong, it is a mistake to defend or justify yourself. You have to pray for forgiveness to the Supreme inside the individual who has been the victim of your wrong action. But if you are doing something right, it is a different matter. If you are attacked, you should always try to be calm, quiet and tranquil within. Peace is the greatest strength. If you have inner peace, then you have a lion's strength.

Spirituality is not the same thing as stupidity. There is no wisdom in surrendering to circumstances and saying, "I am helpless. What can I do?" If you yourself have the power to take action, there is no wisdom in remaining silent and waiting for the person who is harming you or exploiting you to reap his karma. Somebody has deceived you or harmed you, and God has awakened you so that you are aware of it. Now God wants to use you as His instrument to prevent this person from ruining your divine possibilities and, at the same time, to prevent this person from ruining his own divine possibilities by continuing to commit wrong actions. So God wants you to defend yourself; it is your bounden duty to do so.

If you remain silent, the other person will go on exploiting you. You will be continually at his mercy and your own sense of justice will disappear. You have to see the truth as it is, on its own level, and to utilise the truth in its own way. When a new divine thought dawns, you have to use it to build a castle of truth. This is called the sincere approach to reality. Sometimes ignorance cleverly will enter your mind and tell you to wait, since eternity is at your disposal. If you listen to ignorance, you are not defending truth. Truth needs immediate recognition and acceptance. You have to accept the truth and try to manifest the truth. You have to live the divine Truth for only in this way can you justify your own existence and acknowledge your own divine birthright.[237]

Question: How do we know when we should forgive a person who has injured us and when we should defend ourselves?

Sri Chinmoy: There are two types of people. One type is like a monkey or a scorpion. If we allow a monkey to approach us, it will bite and pinch us immediately. If we touch a scorpion, first it will sting our hand. If we touch it again, it will bite us again. So in this world we have to see if someone is constantly trying to destroy us. If ignorance is not decreasing, we have to defend ourselves.

But when the Christ saw that his own people were constantly fighting, he said that there are some people of a good nature whom we should forgive because they sincerely try to do the right thing. If somebody of this type has done something wrong and we forgive him, then he will not do it again because he will know that he has done something wrong. If we tell him, "All right, you have done it. Now do not do it again," he will be ashamed and embarrassed. He will feel repentant that he has done something wrong. Since he has a good nature, he will not do it a second time.

But if somebody has the nature of a scorpion or a monkey, we can give him as many chances as we want, but he will not change his nature. So with him we have to be very strict. If somebody is by nature like a scorpion and we give him a chance, he will simply kill us.[238]

Question: In one meditation, you say that if anybody strikes me on the right cheek, I shall not turn my left cheek to him, because I love him and I don't want him to commit the same mistake again. Do you mean that one can get mad at that person?

Sri Chinmoy: No, it is not that. Let us say that somebody strikes me or does something wrong. Now if I allow that person to do the thing once again, my theory is that in no way will I be helping to perfect him. On the contrary, I am increasing his ignorance. One thing is to forgive and not to take revenge. The saying of Christ from the Bible we all know. I do not want to enter into any controversy. I am only justifying what I have previously written.

Suppose I see that someone has consciously done something wrong and it is damaging him. By doing this wrong thing, he is not, in any way, expediting his spiritual progress or inner progress. On the contrary, I am seeing clearly that he is descending in the scale of evolution. Then what shall I do? In me also is the living God. Now my living God here is acting like a Transcendental Being who is just. It is very easy to forgive someone. But by forgiving him, we have to know whether that person is really going to change his nature. If I just go on saying, "You have done something wrong; you can do more; you are giving me the chance to exercise my compassion," yes, I will exercise my compassion, but in the eyes of God, I will not be allowing him to come to the right path and at the same time, I am wasting my precious life by indulging someone else's wrong action.

So we have to be very careful when somebody does something wrong to us. It is not that we are threatening them. Far from it. Only we have to feel that by allowing him to do the same thing again, or indulge in the same wrong action, we are taking him away from his own divinity.

At each moment, just as we should always try not to do anything wrong ourselves, consciously or unconsciously, we should also not allow another person to do anything wrong. We know that our encouragement of his mistake is in no way serving as a kind of compassion. No. If we encourage him to do the wrong thing again and again, then this is not compassion. This is our self-imposed weakness in the name of compassion.

If somebody attacks, then we have to defend ourselves, because in this self-defense, he will realise that he is striking someone who is innocent, who is crying for light, for reality, for truth. Since we are crying for light, truth, reality and divinity, we have to make the other person feel that only in light will he receive his satisfaction. By striking me, he will not get satisfaction. I tell you a day will come when his soul will come forward and make him feel that he has done something extremely wrong. So if we know that he has done something wrong, then we have to make him understand this, the sooner the better. Then he can enter into the soul's Light and be guided all the time. So this is how I explain this aphorism of mine

During the time of the Saviour Christ, the average man lived in a very undeveloped, semi-animal consciousness. When the Christ instructed people to turn the other cheek, it was in line with His entire teaching of brotherly love, and compassionate kindness. He was trying to teach them mildness and harmlessness, which was very necessary at the time. If he had given them the same instruction that I have given you now, they would not have been able to understand it. They were not sufficiently evolved. Since the average person has evolved considerably in the last two thousand years, we have come to a point where a higher level of teaching can be applied. What the Saviour Christ said was divinely and supremely necessary for the people in his day. I am not saying anything against the Christ or contrary to him. Each spiritual Master teaches according to the level of consciousness of his devotees. Each Avatar is bringing humanity one step higher up the ladder of evolution.[239]

A Poetic View of Forgiveness

My Lord's Name is Forgiveness; my name is hope.

*To forgive the outer world I need peace;
to forgive the inner world I need perfection.*

*Forgiveness is the seeker's immeasurable accomplishment
in both the world of self-giving and the world of God-becoming.*

*Forgiveness is man's happiness-house; forgiveness is God's
Oneness-Home.*

*If you are deplorably weak, then you will sleeplessly remember,
strongly harbour and ceaselessly suffer; if you are soulfully brave,
then you will immediately forgive, completely forget and
unimaginably prosper.*

*Forget the injustice-world; forgiveness-joy will be all yours.
Cry for the world. Look, forgiveness-light is within your
easy reach.
Smile at the world. Look, forgiveness-delight is preceding you
and following you.*

*Forgive the world. The world will sit at your compassion-feet.
Forgive yourself. God will be dancing inside your meditation-
heart.*[240]

Chapter 7

GRATITUDE

Introduction

Just one smile
From my gratitude-heart
Immensely increases
The beauty of the universe.[241]

Absolutely the fastest way to make progress in the inner life is through gratitude.[242]

To feel gratitude means to become a flower in every part of your being — body, vital, mind and heart. Everything in your being will exist as a single, fully-blossomed flower with all its petals completely open. There are thousands of nerves in your body, but these will all disappear and you will feel that you exist only as a most beautiful flower ready to be placed at the Feet of the Supreme. This is gratitude.[243]

Gratitude, gratitude and gratitude: The soul you do not know; the Supreme you do not know. And at this stage in your spiritual development you do not have to know them. But gratitude you do have to know if you want to connect yourself with your own Highest, with the Supreme. If you want to connect yourself with the Real in you, then your gratitude-breath you have to claim as your own, very own.[244]

Pure is our aspiration-plant. Purer is our dedication-flower. Purest is our gratitude-heart. Sweet is our soulful smile.

Sweeter is our inner cry. Sweetest is our gratitude-heart. Gratitude is pure happiness. Happiness is sure perfection. Perfection is complete satisfaction both in man's world and in God's world.[245]

What Is Gratitude?

A gratitude-heart
Is a master key.
It can open
Any heart.[246]

The most important and most significant good quality in our human life is gratitude. Unfortunately, that good quality we somehow manage not to express either in our thoughts or in our actions. Right from the beginning of our life we have somehow learned not to express it. So we have the least amount of the very thing that we need most in order to become a better person.

The things that most deserve our gratitude we just take for granted. Without air we cannot live for more than a minute or two. Every day we are breathing in and breathing out, but do we ever feel grateful to the air? If we do not drink water, we cannot survive. Even our body is composed to a large extent of water. But do we give any value to water? Every morning when we open our eyes, we see the sun blessingfully offering us light and life-energy, which we badly need. But are we grateful to the sun? On the contrary, when the sun is too bright we get mad and complain that it is bothering us.

Every day there are so many people to whom we should offer gratitude. Someone did me this favour. Someone else did me that favour. There is no end to the number of individuals to whom we have to offer our gratitude. If we try to offer gratitude to each individual, it becomes impossible. But no individual created himself. We were all created by God, our Heavenly Father. He is our Source. So if we are not able to offer gratitude to everyone who deserves it from us, we can at least offer gratitude to the Source.

Of course, if we do have the opportunity to offer gratitude to a particular individual, wonderful! But even then what we are really doing is offering gratitude to the Source. Let us say that you do me a favour and I offer you my gratitude. At that time I am actually offering my gratitude to the Inner Pilot, the Source, in you — to the Heavenly Father, who is in you, in me, in the entire creation. The One who deserves my gratitude is not you, but God, our Heavenly Father. He is the very Person who came to you in the form of a good action, and He is the One who is inspiring me to offer you my gratitude. In everything He is the Doer; we are only His instruments.

Outwardly we should try to offer as much gratitude as we can to those who are inwardly or outwardly helping us. I am not saying that we should not offer gratitude to someone if he does something good for us. Far from it! But if we do not have the time to offer our gratitude to everyone who does something for us, God will not blame us. If we cannot offer gratitude to someone individually, no harm. But we have to offer gratitude to the One who has inspired the creation in the form of this human being. To Him we have to offer gratitude. We may not have time to offer our gratitude to the entire creation, but we do have time to offer gratitude to God inside us.[247]

I am speaking about sincere gratitude — the kind of gratitude whose living presence you can only feel inside your heart. If you feel that gratitude is your inner name and also your outer name, if you feel that your only name is gratitude, then immediately your gratitude will jump to the fore and establish its inseparable oneness with your God-oneness-reality.

Gratitude is a most powerful weapon in your life. There is nothing undivine that you cannot get rid of by virtue of the gratitude in your life. Again, there is nothing divine in your life that you cannot increase in boundless measure on the strength of your gratitude. There is only one thing that you need in order to increase your divinity, and that thing is gratitude. If every day you consciously strengthen your gratitude to the Supreme, who is your Guru, my Guru and everybody's Guru, you will see how much progress you will make and how many wrong forces you will be able to get out of your system. I tell you, all the physical, mental and emotional fever that you are suffering from comes from the fact that you have lost your heart's gratitude-breath. If your heart's gratitude-breath is functioning well, then keep it so forever. This is unmistakably the right way to run fast, faster, fastest to the destined Goal.

Gratitude is not a mere word; it is not a mere concept. It is the living breath of your real existence on earth. There is nothing that God will not do for you if you really treasure the gratitude-breath inside your aspiring heart. Please, please, to each and every one of you I am telling this: If you want to run the fastest, then discard the thing that is delaying you. The thing that is making you lame or paralysed in your spiritual life is ingratitude. If you can always maintain your gratitude-breath, then nothing can stand in your way and nobody can prevent you from doing the right thing and becoming the right person: the most perfect instrument of our Lord Beloved Supreme.[248]

Recently, somebody was having difficulty understanding one of my aphorisms about gratitude. The aphorism says, "One second of gratitude to God is worth three hours of intense meditation on God." He thought it meant that just saying "thank you" for one second was worth several hours of meditation. But gratitude is not like shaking hands or saying, "Thank you!" It may take hours, days, months, years or many incarnations to achieve one second of true gratitude. The preparation it takes to come to that stage may take quite a long time. So when I say that gratitude is something most difficult and important, I am referring to this kind of gratitude. When everything of yours has melted and you exist only as a flower ready for worship, when you have placed yourself totally at the Feet of your Beloved Supreme — this is gratitude.[249]

Gratitude is a miracle-action in us. This miracle-action strengthens our physical body, purifies our vital energy, widens our mental vision and intensifies our psychic delight.

The seeker in us tries to be simple, pure, humble, sincere. The easiest and most effective way to cultivate these qualities is to open the gratitude-flower and let it blossom inside our heart petal by petal. How can we do this? Not only do we have to give more importance to what we have, but we also must give all importance to what we do not have.

What we have is wishful thinking, wishful seeking, wishful becoming. Wishful thinking: We think that we shall be great or successful in some way. Wishful seeking: We seek the truth and light in our own way, in the place where we think truth and light must abide. Wishful becoming: We want to become something that pleases us. This is the most deplorable mistake we make. If we want to please ourselves in our own way, then consciously or unconsciously we bring the vital-wolf to the fore.

What we do not have is the breathless inner cry and the measureless outer smile. If we can develop the breathless inner cry, then automatically we develop the measureless outer smile. Either from within we come without, or from without we dive deep within. We can start our journey either from the soul's capacity or from the body's capacity. Ultimately these two capacities have to be united. Needless to say, the soul's capacity is infinitely greater than the body's capacity. But the little capacity that the body has, has to be united with the soul's capacity. The body's greatest capacity is the acceptance of the soul's leadership. If the soul is accepted as the supreme leader, if the soul gets the opportunity to guide, mould and shape our destiny, then we get what we do not have right now: the sweet, pure, breathless, intense inner cry and the sure, measureless outer smile.[250]

Question: Can you say more about what gratitude is and how to express it?

Sri Chinmoy: You do not actually have to try to express gratitude. If you have true gratitude, it will express itself automatically. It will be visible in your eyes, around your being, in your aura. It is like the fragrance of a flower. True, there are some flowers that do not have any fragrance. But in most cases, if there is a beautiful flower, the fragrance will be there naturally. The flower and its fragrance cannot be separated.

Gratitude is the sweetest thing in a seeker's life — in all human life. If there is gratitude in your heart, then there will be tremendous sweetness in your eyes. When I see one of my students, I look at the beauty of his eyes. The beauty of the eyes is determined not by their shape or their colour. No, the beauty of the eyes depends on the heart's beauty. Inside the eyes I look for purity, gratitude and a few other things that come directly from the heart.

But of all the things that I look for, gratitude is the most important. If there is gratitude inside your heart, then it will be expressed through your eyes in the form of sweetness. When some eyes look at me, I see such sweetness in them — like the most delicious Indian sweets.[251]

Question: Is there any relationship between gratitude and humility?

Sri Chinmoy: In the spiritual life two qualities are absolutely of utmost importance. These two qualities are humility and gratitude. If we can add appropriate adjectives to these two words, then they will convey more height and more depth to the seeker in you, the seeker in all human beings. For humility I wish to add 'sincere': sincere humility. For gratitude, I wish to add 'soulful': soulful gratitude.

Gratitude has to be full of the soul-consciousness; otherwise it is not gratitude. Then it becomes a tricky way of gaining something more from the person to whom we show our gratitude. But soulful gratitude is offered to someone for what we have received. Even if that person does not give us anything more in life, not even an iota of joy or love, we shall eternally remain grateful to him for what he has done. We shall always be grateful for the way his gift has added to our life of aspiration, or considerably transformed our life and carried us consciously to the highest Source. When we offer soulful gratitude, it is our eternal recognition of what we have received from someone on our eternal journey across Eternity to Infinity's shore of beauty, light and delight.

The Christ and all spiritual Masters without exception have told us that humility is of constant necessity in order to make the fastest and surest progress in the spiritual life. It is necessary in order to see the Face of our Supreme Beloved, the Inner Pilot. Inner humility and gratitude are our highest achievements. When you feel humble, you feel that your body, vital and mind are responding to your soul's dictates. If you feel grateful, sincerely grateful, soulfully grateful, then you have achieved the highest achievement that the earth-consciousness can offer to the Heaven-consciousness.[252]

Gratitude to God

The seeker's offering
Of an iota of gratitude to God
Is as beautiful as a rose
Held by God in His own Hand.[253]

We are grateful to God, for He is with us here and now. We are grateful to God, for He has created within us a genuine hunger for Him. We are grateful to God, for He has given us a long express train of hope. We are grateful to God, for He has repeatedly told us that He will keep His promise. What is His promise? His promise is that He will not be satisfied unless and until each creation of His satisfies Him in His own Way.

How can we please God in His own Way? First of all, we are not aware of God's Way of operating. Also, we may feel that something will please God, but how can we know if we are correct in our feelings, or whether it is all mental hallucination? There is a way to know whether we are pleasing God in God's own Way. We have to dive deep within and destroy or transform the thought-world and replace it with will-power, adamantine will-power. If we are afraid of God's Will-Power, which is all-powerful, then our life will always remain in untold fear.

We are on earth, here and now, only to please God in God's own Way. It is a difficult task indeed, but we get joy only when we cross hurdles. If we do not cross hurdles, then there will be no lasting reality and there will be no lasting satisfaction. If we do not do everything here and now, then there will be no satisfaction whatsoever, for today's goal is only the beginning of tomorrow's new journey. This new journey and the journey's Goal will come and greet us, for the achievements of the soul and the journey's Goal are inseparable.

When we cry with gratitude, it is the journey's soul that acts in and through us, which is a splendid achievement. And when we smile with gratitude, it is the journey's Goal that has become one with aspiration's starting point and with aspiration's ever-transcending horizon.[254]

Where is our Goal? It is not in the blue skies, it is not in the vast ocean, it is not in the distant desert; it is deep inside us, in the inmost recesses of our heart. Our spiritual heart is infinitely larger than the world. The world grows and flows inside the spiritual heart. If we can feel that our aspiring heart is the living Breath of the Supreme, then we are bound to feel that our cherished Goal is within and not without.

In order to realise the Goal, in order to reach the Goal deep within, we have to renew our life and make it fresh every day. Each day early in the morning we have to revitalise our outer life with golden hope. This hope is not an idle dream; it is the precursor of the divinity which will manifest in and through our outer nature. It is our dynamic divine quality, our golden hope, that sees the Beyond even when it is still a far cry.

To see the Beyond, what is absolutely necessary is our certainty — our implicit faith in ourselves. We have to feel that we are God's chosen child. We have to feel that we embody infinite Light, infinite Truth and infinite Bliss and that now we have to reveal and manifest these divine qualities. Revelation and manifestation are absolutely necessary. The moment we start revealing and manifesting our inner divinity, we will see that we already embody infinite Truth, infinite Light and all the other divine qualities of the Supreme. The supreme Goal is within. The Goal is crying for us, but we are looking for it elsewhere, where it does not exist. We cry for our own existence, which is full of fear, doubt, ignorance, pride, vanity and selfishness. But if we cried for God every day, if we meditated early in the morning for harmony, peace, bliss, plenitude and fulfilment, then only would we see, feel, realise and grow into our Goal. We would discover that our transcendental Goal is within and grow into its very image.

When we reach the transcendental Goal, we see that God and we are one and will forever remain one. Man and God, the aspirant in man and the saviour in God, are totally one. Each fulfils the other. One fulfils through his soul's gratitude; the other fulfils through His Soul's infinite Compassion. Gratitude and Compassion fulfil each other — gratitude from the aspiring soul of man and Compassion from the illumining Soul of God.[255]

Gratitude is one's feeling of concern for the Highest. As the Highest has concern for the lowest, the lowest also should have some concern for the Highest. We may ask, "What can we do for God with our concern?" We have to know what He will think of us if we live an ordinary, undivine, animal life. The answer is that He will feel miserable. He will think that we are not making any progress and are holding back His Manifestation. Our concern for the Highest makes us feel what we can do, and that very thing is to offer gratitude. This is one way of viewing gratitude.

There is another way to view gratitude. When we are about to be totally destroyed, our hope, our pride, everything that we have is shattered and smashed. But inside our utter hopelessness, helplessness, destruction and frustration, if we see a streak of hope, a streak of light, that hope or that light is gratitude. Like a magnet, our iota of light is pulling down a higher force which is entering into us to save us. The moment we have this magnet, it pulls down more of God's Grace and God's Love. The magnet is our inner cry, our gratitude, bringing down more Love from above.[256]

Question: How can I be more thankful to God?

Sri Chinmoy: Just by thinking of gratitude, we cannot become grateful. Our gratitude is like a magnet that pulls God's Compassion down to us. But before our gratitude begins to operate, first God has to pull us towards Him. Once God has started to pull us up, then our gratitude begins to grow and we can pull Him down into us.

There is a special way for a seeker to offer thanks or gratitude to God. It is through cheerfulness, constant cheerfulness. A seeker cannot allow depression to enter into his life of aspiration at any time. He always has to be happy in order to be truly grateful. But if his happiness comes from wallowing in the pleasures of ignorance, that is not the right kind of happiness. Real happiness is something within us which constantly makes us feel that we are expanding our consciousness and wholeheartedly embracing the entire world.

For the seeker, happiness is a feeling of new hope, new life, new dawn, new promise, new achievement. These feelings the seeker has to nourish and treasure within himself. If the seeker in us cherishes these divine qualities, automatically our thankfulness to God will grow; our gratitude-flower will blossom and we will be able to offer it at the Feet of the Lord Supreme.

In spiritual happiness, in the happiness that comes from self-giving and aspiration, gratitude looms large. When we have inner happiness, we do not have to search for gratitude here and there. In our devoted cheerfulness, in our soulful cheerfulness, we are bound to discover constantly increasing gratitude to the Supreme.[257]

Question: How can we offer more gratitude to God?

Sri Chinmoy: We can offer more gratitude to God only by feeling that He is giving us at every moment more and more and more. If somebody gives me a flower, I will offer him my gratitude. If he gives me two flowers, I will give him more gratitude. Then if he gives me three flowers, I will offer him even more gratitude.

In God's case, He wants to give us infinitely more than we need, so naturally our gratitude will increase. But we have to know that He gives everything at His own time and in His own Way — not at our hour or according to our wishes. Our fixed hour is this very moment. But if He gives us something at this moment, then it may create a very serious problem for us. It may increase our ego, pride or vanity or produce many other undivine results. So we can show more gratitude to God by feeling that He is giving us at every moment infinitely more than we need and by offering more of our conscious and sleepless surrender to His Will.[258]

Question: Several times during my working day I take a moment to offer gratitude to God. Is there any special way I should do this?

Sri Chinmoy: This is an excellent thing. When you offer gratitude to the Supreme, try to feel that that gratitude is a world. Your gratitude is tinier than the tiniest, like an ant. But you will try to increase that gratitude into a huge elephant. If you feel that the gratitude-power which you are offering to God is very tiny, absolutely negligible, your feeling is the essence of humility or modesty. But you have to try to grow and expand it. You have to increase your capacity from that of a tiny ant to that of an elephant. Then you will be happy. When your gratitude becomes an elephant, try to have other qualities also. Once it is very huge, vast and strong, inside that powerful elephant try to have all the divine qualities: simplicity, sincerity, purity, humility, oneness, and other divine qualities. At that time, feel that you have all these things inside you.

So, first you have to feel the necessity of making your gratitude-quality large, larger, largest. Then, when you feel that your gratitude has become an elephant, try to see all the divine qualities that you have inside it. All the divine qualities are inside your gratitude-heart. Then you are bound to feel that you are growing into an exemplary instrument of the Supreme. This is how to bring forward all the good qualities that you have. Then you can maintain the highest consciousness all the time while you are at work.[259]

Question: If you have realised the Supreme and become one with the Supreme, is there still gratitude at that time?

Sri Chinmoy: Even if you realise the highest Consciousness, still gratitude will always remain. Gratitude is sweetness and delight. Delight we experience no matter on which plane of consciousness we are. Gratitude is earth's greatest delight and Heaven's greatest delight.

When you have delight and gratitude, at that time you reach the Highest. Just because you have reached the Highest you are happy. If you remain on the highest plane, then you become one with the Vision and one with the Reality. Vision gives capacity to Reality. If this moment Vision is giving something to Reality, although they are one, Reality will naturally feel grateful. When you are on the highest level, Vision and Reality are one. But if you want to play the cosmic Game and you separate the Vision from Reality, then when you have given, naturally, the one to whom you give will express gratitude. But on the highest plane, he who gives and he who receives are one.

Gratitude is in both realisation and manifestation. If you remain in the highest realisation you will be grateful, and if you remain in manifestation you will be grateful. Gratitude has to be constant. Even on the highest plane you have to be grateful.[260]

Cultivating Gratitude

Gratitude-plants
  Grow in Heaven.
Gratitude-flowers
  Grow on earth.
Gratitude-fruits
  Grow inside the heart.[261]

There are two forces: Ingratitude is a destructive force, whereas gratitude is a constructive force. Every day in our multifarious activities, either we express ingratitude or we express gratitude to our fellow beings.

Ingratitude is not our inability to acknowledge the gifts we receive from others. Ingratitude is our deliberate unwillingness to acknowledge the gifts we receive from others. Gratitude is receptivity, the receptivity that acknowledges others' gifts, others' love and concern. Each time we express gratitude, we expand our hearts.

Receptivity can be increased. How can we increase our receptivity? We can increase it by cultivating it. The farmer cultivates the ground and then he sows the seed. He waters it and eventually the seed germinates and grows into a sapling and a tree. Here also, when we cultivate our gratitude-heart, we get the opportunity to sow our pure love there. This pure love grows into true concern, and true concern eventually becomes inseparable oneness.

We receive gifts from our friends in the inner worlds, but we do not want others to know about it. So we speak ill of our inner friends, consciously or unconsciously. We want to make the world believe that we are self-sufficient, but the rest of the world knows that we are receiving something from others. Ingratitude is nothing but a sense of inferiority, an inferiority complex. The gifts we get from others we do not want to acknowledge. We are afraid to expose ourselves to others.

Ingratitude, impurity and the doubting mind go together. It is impurity that divides and separates us and does not allow us to have the feeling of oneness or gratitude. And this impurity unconsciously or consciously is treasured by the doubting mind.

Gratitude, purity and the loving heart always go together. The gratitude-flower grows in our purity-heart. Purity expands our heart. Purity awakens our entire being within to the highest level of consciousness. The heart is self-giving. And what is self-giving today becomes tomorrow God-Delight and God-Perfection.[262]

Question: How can I feel the necessity for gratitude?

Sri Chinmoy: You can feel the necessity for gratitude if you feel that gratitude is your living breath. Feel that if your gratitude-breath is extinguished, then you are dead. Each time you offer gratitude for a fleeting second, feel it is a living breath. On earth there is nothing so important or significant as gratitude. In God's case, the most significant thing He has is Compassion. God is Omnipotent, Omniscient and Omnipresent, but His Compassion-Power makes us close to Him. If He did not have Compassion-Power, we would not care for Him. If we can show God an iota of gratitude, God feels that within us He can exist. Our gratitude is God's Existence, God's House, God's Abode. God has to live in the street unless He can live inside our gratitude-heart.[263]

Question: Is there any specific spiritual discipline that we should practise to make progress on our birthday?

Sri Chinmoy: On that day only offer your gratitude every second, every minute, every hour. If you cannot do it every minute, then every hour try to offer gratitude to the Supreme. If every hour you can offer gratitude, then automatically God will expedite your progress. A birthday is meant for gratitude. Your soul came into the world to do something really great and good for mankind. That opportunity God has given you, and now you are utilising it properly. Because God has given you the opportunity, plus the capacity to fulfil His Dream in and through your life of aspiration and dedication, your gratitude-heart has to come to the fore. Usually, on the physical plane, human beings forget what they have received from God - so much Affection, Love and Compassion, and so many Blessings.

One way that gratitude comes is by being aware of the One who gave you the capacity to continue following the spiritual life. There are millions and millions of people on earth who are not aware of God, who do not believe in God, but you are fully aware of God's existence. Now, your Goal is to realise God and manifest Him here on earth. You are aware of your Goal; you are awakened. For these things, if you can offer gratitude every hour, then it will definitely expedite your inner progress.

There are many, many things you have done which are good, and for that you have to offer gratitude. Again, there are many, many bad things which you have not done. For that also you have to offer gratitude. Just look at your present consciousness. You are on a particular branch of the life-tree. You may not be climbing very fast, but still you are on a branch. There is tremendous opportunity for you to climb up. Here again you can offer gratitude. In so many ways you can offer gratitude to God. For a seeker, a birthday is meant to offer continuous gratitude, so that God can be more pleased and God can use the seeker more confidently and proudly.[264]

Question: How can we be really satisfied with ourselves?

Sri Chinmoy: Unless we offer God our gratitude-tears, we will never be satisfied. Even if God is satisfied, we will not be satisfied with ourselves.

It is difficult for us. Always we take everything for granted. Once we get a mango, we are so satisfied that God has given it to us. God will give unconditionally, but if we pray for the mango, then we will be more satisfied. I prayed; God gave. Everything is mutual. Let us say one leg is gratitude and one leg is compassion, or one eye is gratitude and one eye is compassion. They go together. With one leg, can we walk? With one eye, how far can we see? Both must go together, together.

We have to give God only gratitude-tears, gratitude-tears. We have to say, "God, You have given me the capacity to think of You, to pray to You, to meditate on You, whereas millions and billions of people are not thinking of You, are not praying to You, are not meditating on You."

When gratitude-tears come to the fore in our life, we are satisfied and God is satisfied. If we do not develop gratitude-tears, when God gives something we will be proud and haughty. We will brag: "God has given this blessing to me! God did not give it to him; God did not give it to her." Pride comes to the fore in us. But when we offer gratitude, then our humility comes to the fore. At that time, pride and haughtiness do not enter into the picture.[265]

Question: When we are experiencing delight how can we keep it, and when we are experiencing it, how can we transcend it?

Sri Chinmoy: When we experience delight, we can keep it by offering our soulful gratitude to the Supreme and we can keep transcending it by offering our ever-increasing gratitude to the Supreme.[266]

You may say that it is very difficult to express unconditional gratitude, and you may say that you do not even know what unconditional gratitude is. The meaning of the dictionary word 'unconditional' you do know: without any condition. But the question is, how to practise it in your day-to-day life? I wish you to think of only one thing: joy.

Try to imagine joy in your life. Early in the morning, while you are getting up, just utter the Name "Supreme, Supreme" a few times. Inside your mantra "Supreme," try to feel joy. Imagine at that time that you are drinking something sweet. You are repeating the Name of the Supreme, who is the Source of your life, who is your All. While uttering "Supreme," please try to feel that you are drinking something very sweet and delicious.

When you have sweetness and joy in your mind and in your heart, it becomes easier to offer something unconditionally. Look at a child. He has a beautiful flower in his hand. And what does he do? He comes running towards you and gives you the flower. In return he does not expect anything from you. But why does he come to you? He comes to you because he is happy. There is happiness inside him, spontaneous happiness, and he wants to share that inner happiness with you. But he does not expect anything from you in return — not even a smile. Like that, if we have spontaneous inner happiness, we can offer gratitude to the Supreme.

If we make spiritual progress, then at every moment we can see that there are quite a few divine things we have been doing for years and years. These very things we have been doing precisely because Somebody has been inspiring us. That Somebody is our Lord Supreme. He is inspiring us, He is hoping to create a new world with our dedicated service, and He is promising to Himself at every moment that with our service He will definitely create a new world. He will transform today's world into a world of boundless love, joy and peace.[267]

Results of Gratitude

My gratitude-heart,
Believe it or not,
Has the capacity
To turn all my calamities
Into divine blessings.[268]

My inner strength is founded
  On two things:
God's Forgiveness-Heart
And my gratitude-heart.[269]

Plant gratitude-seeds
  Inside your heart-garden.
Your life will be beautiful
  And fruitful
With glowing deeds.[270]

To see the truth
In its highest form,
We must develop
  A constant
God-gratitude-heart.[271]

Question: Does gratitude help our receptivity during meditation?

Sri Chinmoy: Yes, a gratitude-heart is of paramount importance. You can be most receptive on the strength of your own simplicity, sincerity, purity and humility. When you bring to the fore these divine qualities, which you have inside you, then you can receive the utmost. And inside simplicity, inside sincerity, inside purity, inside humility, you should try to feel a sense of gratitude to your own Inner Pilot. If you have a gratitude-heart, you will be able to receive the utmost. It is a gratitude-heart that can receive from above peace, light and bliss in boundless measure and also manifest them here on earth.[272]

Question: I want to learn from God how to get rid of my depression-hound.

Sri Chinmoy: The quickest way to get rid of your depression-hound is to buy and tame a gratitude-lamb.[273]

Question: Does gratitude cure everything?

Sri Chinmoy: Yes, gratitude cures everything, if inside gratitude there are prayerful tears. If you just say, "I am grateful to you," that gratitude is not deep. It is just like saying, "Thank you very much." But if gratitude comes from the very depths of our being, from the inmost recesses of our heart, because God has done so much for us unconditionally, then there are streaming tears inside that gratitude.

Sometimes if we go one step towards God, He will come ninety-nine steps towards us. Sometimes if we do not take even one step, God comes one hundred steps to awaken us and lift us. At that time, we should develop prayerful tears, saying that we shall become a good person, we shall become a better person and we shall try to please God in His own Way. If we have that kind of gratitude, it will definitely cure all our short-comings and weaknesses in our spiritual life. That kind of gratitude embodies inspiration, aspiration, readiness, willing-ness, self-giving — everything.[274]

Question: Does gratitude have anything to do with joy?

Sri Chinmoy: The best way to establish joy in every part of the being is through constant gratitude to the One who is responsible for our having accepted the spiritual life. At every second we have to bring to our inner mind what we were before we became consciously spiritual. No matter how far away the goal is, we can easily see the distance that we have already covered; in us there is some aspiration, some inner cry, at least some awareness of a higher ideal and goal. We can offer gratitude to God, or to our spiritual teacher, or to our path, or even to our own good qualities that prompted us to enter into the spiritual life.

Again, we can offer gratitude to the inner cry that prompted us to walk along the right path, or to the achievement itself. Gratitude lies in self-giving to the Source, or to the One who has inspired us to see the higher reality and run towards the Goal. We offer gratitude to the Source because it has created in us an inner urge to return to it and seek fulfilment there. And this fulfilment comes only in fulfilling the Source itself. So self-giving in various ways gives us total joy in every part of the being. There is no other way.[275]

Question: How can I know God's Will in my daily life?

Sri Chinmoy: You can know God's Will in your daily life if early in the morning you offer your utmost gratitude to God for what He has already done for you. When you offer your gratitude-heart, then it expands; and when it expands it becomes one with God's universal Reality. The gratitude-heart blossoms like a flower. When the flower is fully blossomed, then you appreciate and admire it.

When your heart of gratitude blossoms, immediately God is pleased. So if you offer gratitude to God for what He has already done for you, then naturally God's sweet Will will operate in and through you. Early in the morning, before you meditate or do anything, offer as much gratitude as possible; offer your soulful tears just because you have become what you are now. If you do this, eventually you will become infinitely more than what you are now. So gratitude will be able to make you feel what God's Will is. God's Will will act in and through you and God will do everything in and through you, and for you, if you offer gratitude.[276]

Gratitude and the Defeat of Undivine Qualities

If even once you have felt the beauty, the purity, the divinity and the reality of gratitude, then definitely something immortal you will feel in yourself. If five years ago you were able to offer gratitude, unconditional gratitude, that very day and time, that very incident, try to imagine.

Nothing can be more meaningful or more fruitful than gratitude in our human life. All our bad qualities, all our undivine qualities, can be washed away and will be washed away by our soulful gratitude. There is no crime in the inner world that cannot be excused by God when He sees that we are offering Him gratitude, most soulful gratitude, for what we are now. We could have been infinitely, infinitely, infinitely worse! And if we offer Him sincere gratitude, then sooner or later, at His choice Hour, He will make us infinitely, infinitely, infinitely better. Only by virtue of our gratitude we will be able to illumine or remove all our dark qualities.

Gratitude is the safest way for us to reach the supreme Destination. The moment we offer our gratitude to the Supreme, many, many undivine forces leave us. Our complaints against our path, against other human beings, even against the Supreme Himself disappear. Our gratitude is infinitely, infinitely more powerful than all the negative forces that either consciously or unconsciously we cherish.

So if you want to get rid of your undivine qualities, you do have to pray and meditate. But along with your prayer and meditation, there is a supreme secret, the secret of secrets, to conquer the undivine qualities that you consciously or unconsciously cherish. You may be displeased with some human beings, displeased with the path, displeased with the Master, even displeased with God Himself. But if you want to make yourself happy, sincerely happy, if you want to grow into happiness, then right from this moment only offer gratitude, gratitude, gratitude to the Supreme; for you are on a spiritual path and you are doing the right thing by offering gratitude. Many, many times you sincerely want to be free from worries, anxieties, jealousies, frustrations and other undivine qualities, but you do not know how you can accomplish this task. I wish to say that sooner than the soonest you can free yourself from those negative forces just by offering gratitude to the Supreme. While offering gratitude to the Supreme, just look around. Where you saw a thick forest, where you saw thorns, there you will see a garden, there you will see flowers.[277]

The Gratitude-Heart

My own gratitude-heart
Is all that matters.[278]

Question: What three qualities are most needed in the spiritual life?

Sri Chinmoy: There is only one quality that we all need. To name three qualities would be redundant. Only one quality can solve all your problems, everybody's problems, and that quality is called a gratitude-heart. Every day count the petals of your gratitude-heart and open another petal. If you want to name the petals, they are simplicity, sincerity, purity, humility, and other divine qualities. Constantly offer your heart of gratitude. That is the only quality that will help you and everyone else solve all problems and also run the fastest. Gratitude embodies all the divine qualities in God's creation. If we are grateful, it is enough.[279]

Our gratitude-heart ceaselessly receives blessingful love, soulful concern and fruitful oneness from above. Our gratitude-heart feels that its very existence on earth is an unconditional act of God's Grace. Our gratitude-heart knows that its acts are for God and for God alone.

In this world we are apt not to value anything or anyone, but our gratitude-heart always values everything in God's creation. It values God the Creator and God the creation. It values God's Compassion and it values God the Compassion. It also values God's Justice-Light and God the Justice-Light, for it knows that God, our Beloved Supreme, is always the Author of all Good.

Our gratitude-heart never fails God. It carries with it flaming aspiration, the burning inner cry and a constant self-giving reality. At every moment God pleases our gratitude-heart with His boundless Concern, Compassion and all-loving Oneness.

We aspire for the Infinite, the Eternal and the Immortal. The seeker in us constantly is trying to transcend himself on the strength of his aspiration-cry and dedication-smile. Our seeker-heart's experience-life, realisation-life and God-fulfilling manifestation-life are clearly read in the Face of our Beloved Supreme. Our own autobiography is clearly read in God's own Face. We offer Him our gratitude-heart and He gives us His constant Assurance that He has chosen us to be His choice instruments, Him to fulfil in His own Way here on earth and there in Heaven.[280]

ABOUT THE AUTHOR

Sri Chinmoy Kumar Ghose was born in the village of
Shakpura, Bengal, India (now Bangladesh), in 1931. He was
the youngest of seven children in a devout family. He spent
the early years of his life in South India, immersed in study
of spiritual disciplines and the humanities. He prayed and
meditated for several hours every day, and had many deep,
inner experiences. He also excelled in several sports.

Heeding an inner command, Sri Chinmoy came to the
United States in 1964, to be of service to spiritual seekers in
the Western world. During the 43 years that he lived in the
West, he served as a spiritual guide to thousands of students in
more than 100 meditation centres worldwide. Sri Chinmoy's
boundless creativity found expression not only in poetry and
other forms of literature, but also in musical composition and
performance, art and sport.

As a peace-lover and peace-dreamer who combined Eastern
spirituality with Western dynamism, Sri Chinmoy became
known as an unparalleled spiritual Master who was dedicated
to the cause of world peace. In 1970, at the invitation of then
Secretary-General U Thant, he began leading twice-weekly
peace meditations for delegates and staff at UN Headquarters.
These continue to this day. He offered hundreds of peace
concerts and university lectures, always free of charge, in the
U.S. and many other countries.

He founded the Sri Chinmoy Oneness-Home-Peace-Run, a
biennial Olympic-style relay in which runners pass a flaming
peace torch from hand to hand as they travel around the globe
bearing the message of universal oneness. He also established
the Oneness-Heart-Tears and Smiles humanitarian organisa-
tion, which serves the less fortunate members of the world
family by supplying food, medical and educational equipment,

and other urgent support.

The luminaries on the international stage who welcomed Sri Chinmoy as their friend include President Mikhail Gorbachev, President Nelson Mandela, Mother Teresa, and Archbishop Desmond Tutu.

On 11 October 2007, Sri Chinmoy passed behind the curtain of Eternity. His spiritual, creative and humanitarian endeavours are carried on worldwide by his students, who practise meditation and strive to serve the world in accordance with his timeless teachings.

ENDNOTES

All books referenced in the preceding text are by Sri Chinmoy. The book title and page numbers are referenced individually for each passage. All, except where noted, are published by Agni Press, 84-47 Parsons Boulevard, Jamaica, New York 11432. All of these books can be found online at www.srichinmoylibrary.com

---

Endnotes for Preface:

[1] *Arise, Awake, Thoughts of a Yogi,* Dec. 14
[2] *Conversations with Sri Chinmoy,* pp.64-65

Endnotes for Body of the Text:

[1] *Seventy-Seven Thousand Service-Trees, Part 41,* #40,629

[2] *Mind-Confusion and Heart-Illumination, Part 2,* p.13

[3] *Service-Boat and Love-Boatman, Part 1,* p. 4

[4] *Mind-Confusion and Heart-Illumination, Part 2,* p.48

[5] *Meditation: Humanity's Race and Divinity's Grace, Part I,* pp. 8-9

[6] *Mind-Confusion and Heart-Illumination, Part 2,* pp.60-61

[7] *The Oneness of the Eastern Heart and the Western Mind, Part 1,* Lecture on "The Inner Hunger," delivered at the University of Dublin, Dublin, Ireland, on 1 July, 1974, pp. 267-268

[8] *Mind-Confusion and Heart-Illumination, Part 2,* pp. 47-48

[9] *Mind-Confusion and Heart-Illumination, Part 2,* p. 14

[10] *Mind-Confusion and Heart-Illumination, Part 2,* p. 29

[11] *Mind-Confusion and Heart-Illumination, Part 2,* p. 13

[12] *Mind-Confusion and Heart-Illumination, Part 2,* pp. 5-6

[13] *Mind-Confusion and Heart-Illumination, Part 2,* p. 27

[14] *Meditation: Man-Perfection in God-Satisfaction (1989 edition),* p. 73

[15] *Mind-Confusion and Heart-Illumination, Part 2,* pp. 34-36

[16] *My Heart-Door I Have Kept Wide Open,* pp. 22-23

[17] *Seventy-Seven Thousand Service-Trees, Part 31,* #30,346

[18] *Two God-Amusement-Rivals: My Heart-Song-Beauty and My Life-Dance Fragrance, Part 7,* #684

[19] *Twenty-Seven Thousand Aspiration-Plants, Part 102,* #10,187

[20] *The Caged Bird and the Uncaged Bird,* p. 82

[21] *Twenty-Seven Thousand Aspiration-Plants, Part 163,* #16,256

[22] *Soulful Questions and Fruitful Answers,* #11

[23] *Sound and Silence, Part 2,* p. 43

[24] *Mind-Confusion and Heart-Illumination, Part 2,* pp.52-54

[25] *The Giver and the Receiver* (Augsburg, Germany: Perfection-Glory-Press, 2002), p. 13

[26] *Seventy-Seven Thousand Service-Trees,* Part 17, #16,360

[27] *A Hundred Years from Now,* p. 22

[28] *Perfection in the Head World,* p. 29

[29] *Illumination-Fruits,* pp. 17-21

[30] *A God-Lover's Earth-Heaven-Life, Part 1,* pp. 28-29

[31] *Earth's Cry Meets Heaven's Smile, Part 3,* p. 282

[32] *My Life's Every Day Hope-Blossoms and Promise-Trees,* #24

[33] *Illumination-Fruits,* p. 24

[34] *Meditations: Food for the Soul,* (Jamaica Hills, Queens, N.Y.: Aum Centre, 1970), aphorism for May 18

[35] *Illumination-Fruits,* pp. 23-24

[36] *A Hundred Years from Now,* pp. 21-22

[37] *Illumination-Fruits,* p. 26

[38] *Ego and Self-Complacency,* p. 24

ᵃaaaa

[39] *Ego and Self-Complacency*, pp. 20-22

[40] *Twenty-Seven Thousand Aspiration-Plants, Part 70, #6983*

[41] *Mother Teresa: Humanity's Flower-Heart, Divinity's Fragrance-Soul, Part 3*, p. 117

[42] *Ego and Self-Complacency*, p. 22

[43] *Sri Chinmoy Answers, Part 29*, pp. 47-48

[44] *Ten Thousand Flower-Flames, Part 96, #9511*

[45] *Four Hundred Gratitude-Flower-Hearts, #71*

[46] *Eternity's Breath*, p. 43

[47] *The Heart-Tears of a God-Seeker*, p. 19

[48] *United Nations Meditation-Flowers and Tomorrow's Noon*, p. 15

[49] *Illumination-Fruits*, pp. 25-26

[50] *Creation and Perfection*, p. 32

[51] *Inner Peace and World Peace*, p. 29

[52] *The Oneness of the Eastern Heart and the Western Mind, Part 3*, Lecture on "Self-Transcendence," delivered at Bakersfield State University, Bakersfield, California, USA, on 30 September, 1978, p. 120

[53] *Illumination-Fruits*, pp. 24-25

[54] *Twenty-Seven Thousand Aspiration-Plants, Part 265, #26,476*

[55] *Everest Aspiration (1978 edition), Talk #46, "Humility and Compassion,"* 16 July 1977, p.102

[56] *Four Hundred Gratitude-Flower-Hearts, #71*

[57] *Illumination-Fruits*, p. 21

[58] *Sri Chinmoy Answers, Part 20*, p. 12

[59] *Canada Aspires, Canada Receives, Canada Achieves, Part 1*, p. 4

[60] *Ego and Self-Complacency*, pp. 20-22

[61] *Perfection and Transcendence*, p. 17

[62] *Two Devouring Brothers: Doubt and Ego*, pp.13-14

[63] *Songs of the Soul*, pp. 85-86

[64] *Canada Aspires, Canada Receives, Canada Achieves, Part 1*, pp. 2-3

[65] *Ten Thousand Flower-Flames, Part 69*, #6877

[66] *Life-Tree Leaves*, p. 23

[67] *Rainbow-Flowers, Part 3*, p. 66

[68] *Illumination-Fruits*, pp. 21-22

[69] *Reality-Dream*, pp. 8-9

[70] *My Christmas-New Year-Vacation-Aspiration Prayers, Part 40*, #24

[71] *Problems, Problems, Are They Really Problems? Part 2*, p. 54

[72] *My Heart-Melody*, pp. 32-34

[73] *Eastern Light for the Western Mind (1972 edition)*, Lecture on "Fear of the Inner Life," delivered at the University of the West Indies, Kingston, Jamaica, on 12 Jan., 1968, p. 6

[74] *My Heart-Door I Have Kept Wide Open*, p. 106

[75] *My Heart-Melody*, pp. 34-35

[76] *Twenty-Seven Thousand Aspiration-Plants, Part 195*, #19,422

[77] *Philosophy: The Wisdom-Chariot of the Mind*, pp. 24-25

[78] *My Heart Shall Give a Oneness-Feast*, p. 15

[79] *Rainbow-Flowers, Part 3*, p. 27

[80] *Silence-Heroes*, #46

[81] *Earth's Cry Meets Heaven's Smile, Part 2* (Santurce, Puerto Rico: Aum Press, 1974) pp. 48-49

[82] *Ten Thousand Flower-Flames, Part 12*, #1111

[83] *Songs of the Soul*, p. 17

[84] *Opportunity and Self-Transcendence*, p. 64

[85] *Sacred Rock Welcomes Sri Chinmoy*, p.25

[86] *Sri Chinmoy Speaks, Part 3*, pp. 62-63

[87] *Sri Chinmoy Speaks, Part 3*, pp. 60-62

[88] *Sri Chinmoy Answers, Part 32*, pp. 14-16

[89] *My Christmas-New Year-Vacation-Aspiration-Prayers, Part 30.* #63

[90] *Inner Progress and Satisfaction-Life,* p. 38

[91] *The Hunger of Darkness and the Feast of Life, Part 1,* pp. 47-50

[92] *Twenty-Seven Thousand Aspiration-Prayers, Part 232,* #23,154

[93] *Father's Day: Father with His European Children,* pp. 33-34

[94] *My Meditation-Service at the United Nations for 25 Years,* pp. 173-174

[95] *Ten Thousand Flower-Flames, Part 37,* #3630

[96] *Two Devouring Brothers: Doubt and Ego,* pp. 59-60

[97] *Sri Chinmoy Answers, Part 22,* pp. 10-12

[98] *Twenty-Seven Thousand Aspiration-Plants, Part 231,* #23,071

[99] *Aspiration-Flow and Dedication-Glow, Part 2,* pp. 4-6

[100] *Fifty Freedom-Boats to One Golden Shore, Part 5,* pp. 37-39

[101] *My Heart's Salutations to Australia, Part 1,* pp. 12-14

[102] *Problems! Problems! Are They Really Problems? Part 2,* pp. 51-52

[103] *Realisation-Soul and Manifestation-Goal,* pp. 36-38

[104] *Sympathy,* p. 29

[105] *The Power of Kindness and Other Stories,* pp. 9-12

[106] *Twenty-Seven Thousand Aspiration-Plants, Part 129,* #12,871

[107] *Ten Thousand Flower-Flames, Part 93,* #9280

[108] *My Christmas-New Year-Vacation-Aspiration-Prayers, Part 44,* #55

[109] *Sympathy,* p. 20

[110] *God's Hour,* (New York: Sky Publishers, 1973), aphorism for March 28

[111] *Illumination-Fruits,* p. 55

[112] *Mother India's Lighthouse* (Blauvelt, New York: Rudolf Steiner Publications, 1973), "Rabindranath: The Myriad-Minded," p. 188

[113] *Silver Thought-Waves, Part 2,* p. 20

[114] *Seventy-Seven Thousand Service-Trees, Part 3,* #2861

[115] *Mind-Confusion and Heart-Illumination, Part 2*, p. 60

[116] *Not Every Day But Every Moment*, p. 56

[117] *Sri Chinmoy Answers, Part 32*, pp. 6-7

[118] *Sri Chinmoy Answers, Part 16*, pp. 3-4

[119] *My Heart-Melody*, pp. 35-36

[120] *Twenty-Seven Thousand Aspiration-Plants, Part 145*, #14,460

[121] *Mind-Confusion and Heart-Illumination, Part 2*, pp. 61-62

[122] *Compassion*, p. 26

[123] *Yoga and the Spiritual Life (1996 edition)*, pp. 15-16

[124] *Mother India's Lighthouse*, "Rabindranath: The Myriad-Minded," (Blauvelt, New York: Rudolf Steiner Publications, 1973), p. 186

[125] *The Hunger of Darkness and the Feast of Light, Part 1*, pp. 60-61

[126] *The Outer Running and the Inner Running*, p. 125

[127] *My Heart-Melody*, pp. 41-43

[128] *Illumination-Fruits*, pp. 3-4

[129] *The Soul's Evolution* (Augsberg, Germany: Perfection-Glory Press, 1999), p. 23

[130] *Flame-Goal*, (Montreal, Canada: Sri Chinmoy Centre, 1973), aphorism for Nov. 2

[131] *Sound and Silence, Part 1*, Lecture on "Compassion," delivered at Brown University, Providence, Rhode Island, USA, on 26 March, 1981, p. 10

[132] *Life-Tree Leaves*, pp. 4-5

[133] *Inspiration-Garden and Aspiration-Leaves*, pp. 23-25

[134] *The Oneness of the Eastern Heart and the Western Mind, Part 2*, Lecture on "Compassion," delivered at Tulane University, New Orleans, Louisiana, USA, on 27 Feb., 1974, pp. 337-338

[135] *My Life's Every Day Hope-Blossoms and Promise-Trees*, #57

[136] *Rainbow-Flowers, Part 3*, p. 34

[137] *Service-Boat and Love-Boatman, Part 1*, pp. 2-3

[138] *Consciousness: God-Journey to Man, Man-Journey to God*, p.59

[139] *Sri Chinmoy Speaks, Part 4*, pp. 38-39

[140] *Rainbow-Flowers, Part 3*, pp. 34-35

[141] *Eternity's Breath*, pp.5-6

[142] *Service-Boat and Love-Boatman, Part 2*, pp. 3-8

[143] *Eternity's Breath*, pp. 7-8

[144] *Service-Boat and Love-Boatman, Part 1*, p. 1

[145] *Ten Thousand Flower-Flames, Part 8*, #42

[146] *The Garden of Love-Light, Vol.1*, #5

[147] *Flame-Waves, Part 1*, pp. 21-22

[148] *Earth's Cry Meets Heaven's Smile, Part 3* (Santurce, Puerto Rico: Aum Press, 1978), p. 203

[149] *Transcendence-Perfection*, #786

[150] *Conversations with Sri Chinmoy*, pp. 66-70

[151] *The Wings of Light, Part 8*, p.43

[152] *The Oneness of the Eastern Heart and the Western Mind, Part 1*, Lecture on "Oneness," delivered at Laval University, Quebec, Canada, on 19 March, 1974, pp. 47-49

[153] *Ten Thousand Flower-Flames, Part 82*, #8,130

[154] *The Oneness of the Eastern Heart and the Western Mind, Part 2*, Lecture on "The Mind-Power Versus the Heart-Power," delivered at Harvard Divinity School, Cambridge, Mass., USA, on 28 May 1975, p. 447

[155] *Conversations with Sri Chinmoy*, page 76

[156] *Twenty-Seven Thousand Aspiration-Plants, Part 53*, #5274

[157] *Rainbow-Flowers, Part 3*, pp. 17-18

[158] *Twenty-Seven Thousand Aspiration-Plants, Part 204*, #20,326

[159] *Arise! Awake! Thoughts of a Yogi* (New York: Frederick Fell, 1972), poem for Aug 17

[160] *The Significance of a Smile*, p. 8

[161] *Two Devouring Brothers: Doubt and Ego*, pp.33-34

[162] *Sri Chinmoy Answers, Part 20*, p. 17

[163] *My Meditation-Service at the United Nations for 25 Years,* p. 116

[164] *Ten Thousand Flower-Flames, Part 81,* #8060

[165] *The Garland of Nation-Souls: Complete Talks at the United Nations* (Deerfield Beach: Florida, Health Communications, Inc., 1995), p. 167

[166] *Sri Chinmoy Speaks, Part 5,* pp. 14-16

[167] *The Garland of Nation-Souls: Complete Talks at the United Nations* (Deerfield Beach: Florida, Health Communications, Inc., 1995), pp. 84-85

[168] *The God of the Mind,* #36

[169] *The Oneness of the Eastern Heart and the Western Mind, Part 1,* Lecture on "Happiness," delivered at Monash University, Melbourne, Australia, on 11 March 1976, p. 14

[170] *Beyond Within (1975 edition),* pp. 403-404

[171] *The Golden Boat, Part 6,* #17

[172] *Service-Boat and Love-Boatman, Part 1,* pp. 2-6

[173] *Twenty-Seven Thousand Aspiration-Plants, Part 69,* #6861

[174] *The Oneness of the Eastern Heart and the Western Mind, Part 3,* Lecture on "Aspiration," delivered at Manhattanville College, *Purchase, New York, USA, on 8 July 1977, U.S.A,* p. 51

[175] *Fortune-Philosophy,* p. 36

[176] *Reality-Dream,* p. 46

[177] *Fifty Freedom-Boats to One Golden Shore, Part 3,* Lecture on "The Spiritual Life," delivered at Iowa Western Community College, Council Bluffs, Iowa, USA, on 3 March, 1974, p. 53

[178] *The Inner Hunger,* p.15

[179] *Mother Teresa: Humanity's Flower-Heart, Divinity's Fragrance-Soul, Part 3,* p. 128

[180] *Father's Day: Father with His European Children,* pp. 44-45

[181] *Sri Chinmoy Answers, Part 1,* pp. 30-31

[182] *Creation and Perfection,* pp. 43-44

[183] *Ten Thousand Flower-Flames, Part 9,* #875

[184] *The Oneness of the Eastern Heart and the Western Mind, Part 1,* Lecture on "My Peace-Life," delivered at the University of Stockholm, Stockholm, Sweden, on 17 July, 1986, pp. 357-358

[185] *Two Devouring Brothers: Doubt and Ego,* p. 14

[186] *Reality-Dream,* pp. 13-14

[187] *God, Avatars and Yogis,* p. 29

[188] *The Heart-Tears of a God-Seeker,* pp.49-51

[189] *My Rose-Petals, Part 7,* Lecture on "Confidence," delivered at Cambridge University, Cambridge, England, on 21 June, 1976, pp. 24-25

[190] *Soulful Questions and Fruitful Answers,* # 17

[191] *Flame-Waves, Part 10,* pp. 13-14

[192] *Art's Life and the Soul's Light,* p.66

[193] *Twenty-Seven Thousand Aspiration-Plants, Part 201,* #20,100

[194] *The Outer Running and the Inner Running (1984 ed.),* pp. 125-126

[195] *Flame-Waves, Part 9,* pp. 22-23

[196] *Twenty-Seven Thousand Aspiration-Plants, Part 78,* #7768

[197] *The Oneness of the Eastern Heart and the Western Mind, Part 3,* Lecture on "Desire versus Aspiration," delivered at Cornell University, Ithaca, New York, USA, on 16 March, 1989, p. 235

[198] *Wisdom-Waves in New York, Part 1,* Lecture on "The Desiring Man, the Aspiring Man and the Self-Giving Man," delivered at Union College and University, Schenectady, New York, USA, on 4 March, 1978, p. 9

[199] *Fifty Freedom-Boats to One Golden Shore, Part 3,* Lecture on "The Human and the Divine," delivered at the University of South Alabama, Mobile, Alabama, USA, on 27 Feb. 1974, p. 31

[200] *The Oneness of the Eastern Heart and the Western Mind, Part 1,* Lecture on "The Eternal Seeker," delivered at the Australian National University, Canberra, Australia National Territory, on 6

March 1976, p. 8

[201] *The Oneness of the Eastern Heart and the Western Mind, Part 1,* Lecture on "Beauty," delivered at McMaster University, Hamilton, Ontario, Canada, on 24 March, 1974, p. 69

[202] *God and the Cosmic Game,* pp. 29-30

[203] *Sri Chinmoy Answers, Part 13,* p. 12

[204] *Twenty-Seven Thousand Aspiration-Plants, Part 69,* #6865

[205] *The Oneness of the Eastern Heart and the Western Mind, Part 2,* Lecture on "Realisation," delivered at the University of New Mexico, Albuquerque, New Mexico, USA, on 24 April, 1974, p. 414

[206] *Everest-Aspiration (1978 edition), Talk #70,* "I Was a Student of Prayer," 18 July, 1977, pp. 139-140

[207] *Everest-Aspiration (1978 edition), Talk #76,* "My Divine Pilgrimage," 18 July 1977, pp. 149-150

[208] *Aspiration-Glow and Dedication-Flow, Part 1,* pp. 11-13

[209] *My Meditation-Service at the United Nations for 265 Years,* p. 11

[210] *The Oneness of the Eastern Heart and the Western Mind, Part 1,* Lecture on "Service," delivered at the Sir Wilfred Laurier University, Waterloo, Ontario, Canada, on 26 March 1974, pp. 79-80.

[211] *The God of the Mind Songbook,* #10

[212] *The Oneness of the Eastern Heart and the Western Mind, Part 1,* Lecture on "Force," delivered at the University of Swansea, Swansea, Wales, on 17 July 1974, p. 406

[213] *Aum Magazine, Vol. II-2, #9,* Sept. 27, 1975

[214] *Rainbow-Flowers, Part 3,* pp. 28-29

[215] *Flame-Waves, Part 4,* pp. 43-44

[216] *Sri Chinmoy Speaks, Part 8,* pp. 52-54

[217] *The Soul's Special Promise, Part 2,* pp. 27-28

[218] *Sri Chinmoy Answers, Part 17,* pp. 7-8

[219] *My Christmas-New Year-Vacation-Aspiration-Prayers, Part 20,* #76

[220] *You Belong to God*, pp. 109-111

[221] *Oneness-Reality and Perfection-Divinity*, pp.25-26

[222] *My Bondage-Life Is My Self-Invention*, #31

[223] *Sri Chinmoy Answers, Part 24*, pp. 10-11

[224] *Aspiration-Glow and Dedication-Flow, Part 2*, pp. 53-54

[225] *Earth's Cry Meets Heaven's Smile, Part 3*, (Santurce, Puerto Rico: Aum Press, 1978), p. 204

[226] *Great Masters and the Cosmic Gods*, pp. 20-21

[227] *Bela Chale Jai Songbook*, #25

[228] *Khama Karo* (Zurich, Switzerland: Madal Bal Publications, 1998), pp. 18-22

[229] *Aum Magazine, Vol. II-2*, #9, Sept. 27, 1975

[230] *Conversations with Sri Chinmoy*, pp. 39-41

[231] *What I Need from God*, pp. 17-19

[232] *Sri Chinmoy Answers, Part 33*, pp. 35-36

[233] *Ten Thousand Flower-Flames, Part 5*, #446

[234] *Sri Chinmoy Answers, Part 22*, pp. 46-49

[235] *God and the Cosmic Game*, p. 13

[236] *Twenty-Seven Thousand Aspiration-Plants, Part 2*, #163

[237] *My Meditation-Service at the United Nations for 25 Years*, pp. 286-287

[238] *The Significance of a Smile*, pp. 46-47

[239] *Earth's Cry Meets Heaven's Smile, Part 3* (Santurce, Puerto Rico: Aum Press, 1978), pp. 266-268

[240] *Four Hundred Gratitude-Flower-Hearts*, #66

[241] *Twenty-Seven Thousand Aspiration-Plants, Part 179*, #17,869

[242] *My Weightlifting Tears and Smiles, Part 1*, p. 72

[243] *My Meditation-Service at the United Nations for 25 Years*, p. 314

[244] *Sri Chinmoy Answers, Part 1*, p. 61

[245] *Wisdom-Waves in New York, Part 1*, Lecture on "Gratitude-

Heart," delivered at the State University of New York at Platts-burgh, New York, USA, on 18 March, 1978, p. 23

[246] *Ten Thousand Flower-Flames, Part 10,* #969

[247] *My Heart Shall Give a Oneness-Feast,* pp. 32-34

[248] *Sri Chinmoy Answers, Part 1,* pp. 59-61

[249] *My Meditation-Service at the United Nations for 25 Years,* p. 314

[250] *Everest-Aspiration (1978 ed.), Talk # 2,* "Gratitude," pp. 3-4

[251] *Sri Chinmoy Answers, Part 5,* p. 1

[252] *The Significance of a Smile,* pp. 24-25

[253] *Ten Thousand Flower-Flames, Part 7,* #678

[254] *Everest-Aspiration (1978 edition),* Talk #65, "Gratitude," 18 July 1977, pp. 130-131

[255] *A Hundred Years from Now,* pp. 14-16

[256] *Illumination-Fruits,* pp. 13-14

[257] *Canada Aspires, Canada Receives, Canada Achieves, Part 1,* pp. 7-9

[258] *Niagara Falls vs. Children's Rise,* pp. 1-2

[259] *The Inner World and the Outer World (1999 ed.),* pp. 62-63

[260] *The Significance of a Smile,* pp. 29-30

[261] *Seventy-Seven Thousand Service Trees, Part 49,* #48,465

[262] *My Rose-Petals, Part 6,* pp. 37-39

[263] *The Significance of a Smile,* pp. 27-28

[264] *The Soul's Special Promise: Answers to Questions on Birthdays and the Soul, Part 2,* pp. 4-6

[265] *Only Gratitude-Tears,* pp. 18-19

[266] *At the Doors of Time and Delight Opportunity Knocks,* p. 4

[267] *Live in the Eternal Now,* pp. 83-85

[268] *Twenty-Seven Thousand Aspiration-Plants, Part 241,* #24,078

[269] *Each Hour Is a God-Hour,* #45

[270] *Twenty-Seven Thousand Aspiration-Plants, Part 145,* #14,406

[271] *Seventy-Seven Thousand Service-Trees, Part 28,* #27,090

[272] *My Meditation-Service at the United Nations for 25 Years,* p. 315

[273] *Soulful Questions and Fruitful Answers,* #59

[274] *My Heart-Melody,* pp. 8-9

[275] *Flame-Waves, Part 8,* pp. 37-38

[276] *Father's Day: Father with His European Children,* pp. 32-33

[277] *Live in the Eternal Now,* pp. 86-88

[278] *Impossibility Bows Songbook,* Song #26

[279] *The Inner World and the Outer World* (Augsburg, Germany: Perfection-Glory-Press, 1999), pp 67-69

[280] *Wisdom Waves in New York, Part 1,* Lecture on "Gratitude-Heart," delivered at the State University of New York at Plattsburgh, New York, USA, on 18 March, 1978, pp. 23-24

Made in the USA
Middletown, DE
07 June 2023

32242942R00106